The Power of Play

Also by David Elkind

The
Power of
Play

How Spontaneous,
Imaginative Activities
Lead to Happier,
Healthier Children

David Elkind, PhD

Da Capo Lifelong Books
A Member of the Perseus Books Group

Designed by Brent Wilcox
Set in 10.75 point Berkeley by the Perseus Books Group

Library of Congress Cataloging-in-Publication Data
Elkind, David, 1931-
    The power of play : how spontaneous, imaginative activities lead to happier, healthier children / David Elkind.
        p.   cm.
    Includes bibliographical references and index.
    ISBN-13: 978-0-7382-1053-7 (hardcover : alk. paper)
    ISBN-10: 0-7382-1053-6 (hardcover : alk. paper)
    1. Play—Psychological aspects.   I. Title.
    BF717.E397 2007
    155.4'18—dc22

                                                                                                2006035592

Published by Da Capo Press
A Member of the Perseus Books Group
http://www.dacapopress.com

Da Capo Press books are available at special discounts for bulk purchases in the U.S. by corporations, institutions, and other organizations. For more information, please contact the Special Markets Department at the Perseus Books Group, 11 Cambridge Center, Cambridge, MA 02142, or call (800) 255-1514 or (617) 252-5298, or e-mail special.markets@perseusbooks.com.

10 9 8 7 6 5 4 3 2 1

To my granddaughters
Lily, Heather, and freshly minted Maya,
and to the latest generation of nieces and great nieces,
Hallie, StellaBlue, and Raven,
for the fresh joy and excitement they have brought into our
lives and for reinforcing my belief in the power of play.

Contents

Introduction

Children's play—their inborn disposition for curiosity, imagi-nation, and fantasy—is being silenced in the high-tech, commercial-ized world we have created. Toys, about which children once spun elaborate personal fables, now engender little more than habits of pas-sive consumerism. The spontaneous pickup games that once filled neighborhoods have largely been replaced by organized team sports and computer games. Television sitcoms and movie CDs have all but eliminated the self-initiated dramatic play that once mimicked (and mocked) the adult world. Parents, anxious for their children to suc-ceed in an increasingly competitive global economy, regard play as a luxury that the contemporary child cannot afford.

Over the past two decades, children have lost twelve hours of free time a week, including eight hours of unstructured play and outdoor activities. In contrast, the amount of time children spend in organized sports has doubled, and the number of minutes children devote to passive spectator leisure, not counting television but including sports viewing, has increased fivefold from thirty minutes to over three hours.[1] The disappearance of play from the lives of our children is mirrored in the media. Television programs rarely depict children as simply playing and having a good time. More often they are portrayed as high-achieving miniadults or as preoccupied with school issues or family problems such as divorce, substance abuse, AIDS, and job loss. Even the cartoons have changed. Fred Flintstone and George Jetson never let work get in the way of having fun. Bob the Builder and SpongeBob SquarePants, on the other hand, love their jobs. Sponge-Bob was even named Employee of the Month at the fast food restaurant where he works. When did life for a child get to be so hard?

The health consequences for children resulting from the disappearance of play are already apparent. At the first ever Surgeon General's Conference on Children's Mental Health in 2000, it was reported that "growing numbers of children are suffering needlessly because their emotional, behavioral and developmental needs are not being met by the very institutions that were explicitly created to take care of them."[2] Over 20 percent of the child population now suffers from these problems. Moreover, the surgeon general also suggests that two-thirds of the children in this country suffer at least one health problem. Thirteen percent of our children are obese. We have more than 2 million children on Ritalin and other ADHD (Attention Deficit Hyperactivity Disorder) medications. This may be the first generation of American children who are less healthy than their parents.

The psychological consequences of the failure to engage in spontaneous, self-initiated play are equally serious and equally worrisome. Because children are spending so much time in front of television, as well as other screens, there is little time for exercising their predisposition for fantasy, imagination, and creativity—the mental tools required for success in higher-level math and science. The failure to develop these tools is, in part at least, one of the reasons America is falling behind other countries in attracting young people into these fields. For example, enrollment in U.S. science and engineering graduate education peaked in 1993, declined through 1998, and rose to a near record level by 2001. Graduate enrollment in engineering and computer science drove the recent growth, *mostly because of foreign students*. Enrollment in most other science fields remained level or declined.[3]

Our schools are now contributing to the suppression of curiosity, imagination, and fantasy. Growing numbers of elementary schools are eliminating recess in favor of more time for academics. Our increasingly test-driven curricula have all but eliminated creative and playful teaching practices. Increasingly, rote learning methods are used to prepare children for the all too frequent assessments. Brazilian educator Paulo Freire wrote that education either liberates or domesticates. Colonial powers once used rote learning methods to domesticate indigenous peoples and induce obedience to external authority. Rote learning is anathema to critical, innovative thinking.

All of these concerns explain why I wrote this book. A quarter of a century ago I wrote a book entitled *The Hurried Child*. At that time I was working as a clinician as well as a college professor. I was increasingly concerned with the mental health problems I saw in my young patients, who were being pressured to grow up too fast, too soon. *The Hurried Child* was written to alert parents and educators to risks involved in hurrying children. Since that book was written, I have given up most of my clinical work and and have involved myself with broad issues that affect the family and children. In a book published more than a decade later, *Ties That Stress*, I tried to highlight a larger problem—a troubling need imbalance in our society between the needs of children and those of adults.[4] Up to the middle of the twentieth century, the need imbalance favored children and adolescents. During the second half of the twentieth century and continuing into the twenty-first, the imbalance has shifted in favor of parents and adults.

Consider the fact that children are now regarded as consumers, a niche population to be targeted directly without concern for parental approval of the advertised product. High-fat, high-sodium foods, sugary soft drinks, disposable fad toys, and much more, are marketed directly to children. Quality television programming for children, which brings relatively low revenue for the producers, is only a small part of contemporary TV fare. And the programming at family hours is increasingly foul-mouthed, overtly sexual, and/or violent. Many computer games for children are equally inappropriate. Clearly some adults are putting the profit motive ahead of children's needs. What I did not fully appreciate when I wrote *Ties That Stress* was an unintended consequence of this new needs imbalance—the silencing of children's play. All too often children's need for play is exploited and redirected to serve commercial ends. All too often children's spontaneous active play has been transformed into passive audience participation.

In regard to the role of play in child development, I always assumed that children used play to nourish their cognitive, social, and emotional development. But I never made an effort to articulate how play contributes to healthy development at successive age levels. I now appreciate that silencing children's play is as harmful to healthy development (if not more so) as hurrying them to grow up too fast too soon. To bring this point home with as much force as I can, I have articulated a developmental theory of play that was implicit in much of my earlier work but wasn't spelled out. In this theory, as in most of my writing, I have tried to unite Freud's motivational orientation with the intellectual approach of Jean Piaget. It is this intellectual/motivational theory of play development that informs the entire book. I will present my theory in Chapter 1 and then highlight social developments that have worked against children's engaging in healthy play. I want to clarify—to parents, educators, and legislators—the central role of play in healthy intellectual, social, and emotional development. Finally I want to share with parents and educators suggestions for bringing spontaneous, self-initiated play back into children's lives.

David Elkind, October 2006
East Sandwich, MA

I The Changing World of Play

one

Play, Love, and Work: An Essential Trio

Play is the answer to the question, How does anything new ever come about? —JEAN PIAGET

Freud was once asked what he thought was necessary to lead a happy and productive life. He replied, "Lieben und Arbeiten," loving and working. With all due respect to Freud, I believe he should have included "Spielen," playing. Love, work, and play are three inborn drives that power human thought and action throughout the life cycle. Play is our need to adapt the world to ourselves and create new learning experiences. An infant who brings a rattle close enough to look at it has created a fresh learning experience. Loving is our disposition to express our desires, feelings, and emotions. From an early age, infants communicate their needs through their distinct cries. Work is our disposition to adapt to the demands of the physical and social worlds. An infant easily adapts to the shape of the nipple and pacifier. Initially play, work, and love function together as a single disposition. During the course of development, however, play, love, and work become increasingly separated and individuated, and the role of these drives changes over time.

It is important at the outset to correct a common misunderstanding about work and play. Work is often associated with pain, and play with pleasure. I am arguing here, however, that play, love, and work are separate drives. Play when divorced from work can be painful. Consider a teacher who has innovative ideas about how to make the subject matter interesting and exciting for his students. If that teacher cannot implement his ideas, thanks to a test-driven curriculum, he will be frustrated and unhappy. Contrariwise, a worker whose ideas are welcomed and rewarded by her employer is going to feel happy at work. Brought together, play and work are pleasurable; it is only their separation that is painful. And play, in the absence of love and work, is simply entertainment.

The idea that play is a basic, vital human disposition has long been recognized. Philosopher Friedrich Schiller regarded play as crucial to the human experience.[1] For Schiller, play allows humans to realize their highest aspirations and ideals. Other writers have defined play as a major dynamic in linguistics,[2] literature,[3] and game theory.[4] These writers, however, treat play in isolation from love and work, and apart from child development. Psychologists and educators have also studied and written about play apart from the other dispositions.[5]

To fully appreciate the power of play, I believe we need to see how it develops in relation to love and work. The major stages of child development have traditionally been described in terms of the physical, intellectual, and emotional-social development occurring in each period. In this book I will describe the major eras of development from the standpoint of the interaction of play, love, and work. In this integration I intend to show how play, love, and work complement, not oppose, each other during each major phase of growth. Further, when play, love, and work are all involved, learning and development are the most effective. Play is not a luxury but rather a crucial dynamic of healthy physical, intellectual, and social-emotional development at all age levels.

Play, love, and work are operative throughout the human life cycle. The relative contribution of each disposition, however, varies with the particular stage of growth. The development of play, love, and work unfolds in four major periods. During infancy and early childhood, play is the dominant and directing mode of activity; love and work are secondary. After the age of six or seven—during childhood proper— work takes charge as play and love take on supportive roles. In adolescence love becomes the overriding determinant of activity, with work and play subsumed under this disposition. In adulthood, play, love, and work become fully separate but can appear together in one or another combination. Some adults, for example, love their work but have little time for play. Then there are the professional athletes whose play *is* their work. And sometimes all of us appreciate play, love, and work as a single, joyful experience.

Infancy and Early Childhood

During infancy (roughly the first two years of life) play, love, and work are almost indistinguishable, with play being the most central. The infant's curiosity and interests determine what activities the infant needs to engage in and what he will create, learn, and enjoy. At this stage the child is recreating reality—a reality already known to older children and adults. He is not only creating that reality (play) but adapting to a new reality (work). By the end of the first year of life, the infant has created the notion of a *permanent object* (an object believed to exist when it is no longer present to the senses). Now the infant cries when the mother disappears because he has a mental representation of the absent parent. The infant also uses this new mental creation to accommodate to the external world. Once the concept of a permanent object is attained, the infant will look for objects that are hidden and shows pleasure in retrieving hidden objects. Play, love, and work are thus woven together in the infant's initial interactions with the world.

In early childhood (roughly 2–6 years) play, love, and work become slightly separated but are still closely linked. At this stage children are able to both learn and create symbols. Children will learn the names of people, places, and things, as well as numbers and letters. In so doing they are adapting to the demands of the environment—working. But young children often create their own words, which they use as if they were equally learned from the environment. For example, my granddaughter Lily calls her grandmother "Mimi," but we have no idea where that name came from. Lily uses this word as if it had come from us, not her. The young child's creation of new words is a good example of how a personal creation (derived from play) can also be a practical adaptation (function as work).

In addition to creating their own names for things, children create their own concepts, which they also name. When he was four, my oldest son began using the word "stocks." I thought this precocious and already had him enrolled in the Harvard Business School on his way to a seat on the New York Stock Exchange. It turned out, however, that he had created the word "stocks" to describe his mother's stockings and my socks. It was creative but also adaptive in that it allowed him to unite two groups of things in a single concept. As for love, young children generally take great pleasure in creating and using new words, symbols, and drawings.

When young children create a new word, they use it as if everyone understood it. The young child still does not clearly distinguish what comes from within and what comes from without. This is true for both play and nonplay experiences. When another of my sons was a preschooler, he had a toothache and I asked him if it hurt very much. He looked rather annoyed at me and replied, "Yes, can't you feel it?" Children's play creations are realities for them, and they expect us to treat their imaginary companions as real. Young children get upset if we dismiss or treat lightly their play creations.

Play, then, is the dominant and directing mode of learning during this age period, and children learn best through self-created learning experiences. This was understood by those who invented early childhood education. Friedrich Froebel, the creator of the kindergarten, gave young children twenty "gifts," open-ended craft projects that allowed children to create their own realities with a variety of plastic materials.[6] Maria Montessori introduced what she called "auto-didactic materials" that children could master through trial and error, insight, and hypothesis testing.[7] Certainly young children can learn the names of numbers and letters and even sight-read a few words. But this is work and should make up only a small part of an overall hands-on, self-directed early childhood curriculum.

The Elementary School Years (Ages 6–12)

During the elementary school years the disposition to work (adapt to the external world) becomes the child's primary dynamic. This may be one reason that Freud spoke of this period as the *latency* stage, in which the sexual drive is relatively quiet.[8] During the early elementary years children (roughly ages 6–8 or 9) learn the basic tool skills of reading, writing, arithmetic, and computing. The emphasis during this stage is on adapting to the demands of the social world. But learning the tool skills is less onerous if a playful element is present. That was the genius of author Dr. Seuss (Theodor Seuss Geisel). He appreciated that young children learn best through rhyme, rhythm, and repetition. Consider the following from *Hop on Pop*.[9]

ALL	BALL
BALL	WALL
We all play ball	Up on a wall

Likewise, learning basic arithmetic can be easier and more fun if it involves a play element. That is why manipulatives like rods of different length, beads, and unit blocks are so valuable. These materials allow children to use their imagination to learn numbers. If they have the image of the rods or beads or blocks in their head, they can begin to manipulate them mentally. This is the forerunner of the mental manipulation of actual numbers. Even at this stage children resist rote learning and want to understand, not just repeat and imitate. The young child's curiosity, however, is not always appreciated. The following humorous but sad example of bad teaching is from the memoir *Angela's Ashes*.

> Question Quigley raises his hand. We call him Question Quigley because he is always asking questions. He can't help himself. "Sir," he says, "what's Sanctifying Grace?" The master rolls his eyes to heaven. He is going to kill Quigley. Instead, he barks at him. "Never mind what Sanctifying Grace is, Quigley. That's none of your business. You are here to learn the Catechism and do what you are told. You are not here to be asking questions. There are too many people wandering around the world asking questions and that is what has us in the state we are in and if I find a boy in this class asking questions, I won't be responsible for what happens. Do you hear me, Quigley?"[10]

Teachers are all-important at this stage and can encourage or discourage a child's attitude toward learning. Affection for a teacher at this stage facilitates learning, just as dislike for a teacher can inhibit it. As a young boy learning Hebrew after school, I had a teacher much like the master described above. And, like Question Quigley, I was always asking questions. We were taught to read Hebrew without understanding it. I kept asking what the words meant but never got an answer. I finally became disgusted and quit Hebrew school, much to the unhappiness of my parents. After that early experience, I never had an interest in learning a foreign language. It was only after I studied with Swiss psychologist Jean Piaget that I was motivated to learn French.

During the latter years of childhood (ages 8–12) children learn about the larger social, physical, and scientific worlds. The curriculum of the late elementary school years focuses on making the unfamiliar world familiar. Children at this age learn about people and countries other than their own. They also learn about the earth and the planets. In beginning science they learn elementary principles of physics, chemistry, and biology. They participate in more advanced forms of art, music, and sports. Again, the subject matter can be taught in ways that are interesting and fun. For example, children will be more interested and get more out of a chemistry or physics project if it is taught with a problem-solving or discovery method.

At this developmental age, play becomes more prominent than it was during the preceding period. Games with rules are the major form of play during the late elementary years, and friends rather than parents become the most desired playmates and companions. It is through creating their own games with rules that children learn important social skills, attitudes, and values. With respect to love, the purported latency of the sex drive does not preclude the child's forming emotional attachments to friends. The child's feelings of affection for friends encourage peer social learning. At this stage, play and love facilitate adaptation to the world. That is why children who don't like their teachers and/or have few friends may have more difficulty learning than do children with positive relationships.

Adolescence

With the advent of puberty and its accompanying physical, psychological, and emotional changes, love becomes the dominant predisposition. It often preoccupies young adolescents to the extent that they have little interest in academic work or play. Toward the end of this period, the love can be invested in both work and play as young people pair off and love is attached to a particular person. At this stage young people start thinking about their future educational and occupational options.

When the young person enters early adolescence (roughly ages 12–15), the love disposition takes center stage, and learning and playing take a subordinate role. Freud said this is the age when the Oedipal conflict (the love of the child for the parent of the opposite sex) reawakens. Now the young person must begin the search for a substitute love object. The resulting change in priorities among the three dispositions helps account for the seventh grade slump—declining interest in academics during the first years of puberty. If we were wise, we would do away with seventh grade and instead have young people put on a play, build a boat, or set up a store for learning basic relationship and coping skills. Such projects would bring together the three dispositions in an age-appropriate way.

During late adolescence (roughly ages 16–19) play, love, and work reach a kind of equilibrium. Young people have done their initial sexual exploration and the peer group loses its power. Adolescents begin to pair off and establish more lasting love relationships. This attaches the love disposition to a particular person of the opposite or same sex and to a small group of select friends. There is a new attachment to career paths and/or educational goals that leads to a fresh interest in learning. Play becomes more institutionalized as young people realize their creative potential by engaging in the performing or creative arts, for example, playing in bands, acting in plays, or writing. At this stage young people begin to be creative in the social sense as their creations can be appreciated and valued by the larger society.

Adulthood

When the period of physical growth ends, young people enter the adult years, when the dispositions of play, love, and work are fully separated. Play is now primarily a means of recreation, a reprieve from the world of work. In this new role, play loses some of the creative functions it performed for children. Yet many adults bring the creative impulse to their work or at least to their hobbies and avocations. Creative cooking, needlepoint, carpentry, gardening, and pottery making are a few examples. These creative outlets are often pleasurable and so bring in the love disposition. The end result of this union of play and love is often a product that can be of use in the real world—a work product. Avocations of this kind enable adults to once again bring the dynamisms of play, love, and work into a single integrated activity.

Once we are grown, marriage and family relationships become the focus of our love. Although based on love, lasting relationships require work: adaptation to the needs and desires of the other person. They also require learning about ourselves and the other person. Lasting relationships also require playfulness and a sense of humor, which keep us from taking ourselves too seriously and enable us to enjoy our relationship. With the birth of children, love is coupled with the work but also the pleasure and joy of parenting. Again, a sense of humor and a playful attitude make parenting more enjoyable for both parents and children. Fortunately our children often show us the way to be playful. I wrote this book partly to help parents appreciate how humor and playfulness contribute to the well-being of children—and parents as well.

In adulthood work, like play, can be isolated from the other dispositions. For too many people, work is just something they do to earn a living; it affords them little in the way of creative challenge or emotional satisfaction. Yet individuals can make even the lowliest occupation a work of love. The missionary nun Mother Theresa was a case in point. She cared for the "poorest of the poor" out of a feeling of love and devotion. This is far different from carrying out tasks only because one is paid to do them.

As I suggested above, adults have the potential to reunite the dynamisms of play, love, and work. Philosopher-psychologist Mihaly Csikszentmihalyi describes a special instance of this adult union of play, love, and work as *flow*.[11] A personal example may help illustrate what he means. Although I had no name for it at the time, I have experienced flow. On rare occasions when I am sailing on my small catboat, the winds are fair, the sail is full, I am heeling at just the right angle, and the boat seems to sing as it moves forward in what feels like an effortless movement. I feel like part of the boat and we are both part of the sea. The feeling is sheer joy. Thanks to Mihaly, I now know that what I experienced was flow. Flow always has its chance elements (the wind and current in my example), which prevents it from being a common experience.

Mihaly identified flow when he was asking people to talk about feelings of enjoyment. He reports:

Athletes, artists, religious mystics, scientists and ordinary people described their most rewarding experiences with very similar words. And the description did not vary much by culture, gender, or age. Old and young, rich and poor, men and women. Nine elements were mentioned over and over again when people are experiencing a truly enjoyable experience:

1. There are clear goals every step of the way
2. There is immediate feedback on one's actions
3. There is a balance between challenges and skills
4. Action and awareness are merged
5. Distractions are excluded from consciousness
6. There is no worry of failure
7. Self-consciousness disappears
8. The sense of time becomes distorted
9. The activity becomes autotelic (an end in and of itself)

I watched ice skaters, skiers, and snowboarders compete at the 2006 Olympic Games, and the ones who succeeded seemed to be in a state of flow, performing difficult feats effortlessly and gracefully. The experience of flow is an exceptional instance of what I refer to as the integration of play, love, and work. In adults flow does not happen unless we actively strive to unite these dynamisms in the ways described above. Flow can occur in our avocations, jobs, or relationships. And it can happen to us as parents. Sometimes when we say or do just the right thing, and our child beams back at us in a happy and loving way, we know the joy of flow.

In many ways, the changing world of toys, described in the next chapter, keeps children from experiencing the sense of flow.

two

Toys Aren't Us

Children learn about themselves and their world through their play with toys. In the past half century, mass production has made inexpensive toys available in enormous quantities and seemingly unlimited variety. Even low-income children today have more toys than children of earlier generations. Once given to celebrate birthdays and Christmas, toys are now routinely purchased all year long. There has been a quality change as well. The majority of toys are now made of plastic. These playthings generally lack the warmth of wood, the texture of natural fabrics such as cotton or wool, or the solidity of metal. Children's playthings are also more automated than they were in the past. Windup, spring-loaded toys were the earliest of this genre. Now toys containing embedded computer chips can recognize a child's voice, react with emotions from surprise to dismay, and respond to specific words a child says. All of these changes have impacted the personal and social skills, attitudes, and values children acquire from toy play.

Changes in the Personal Benefits of Toy Play

Too Many Toys, Too Often

Toy play is one of the ways in which children nurture their disposition for imagination and fantasy. Like other human potentials, imagination and fantasy can only be fully developed through practice. Yet the sheer number of toys owned by contemporary children weakens the power of playthings to engage children in dramatic thinking. Abundance, like familiarity, breeds contempt. My preschool granddaughter doesn't really value her toys because she has so many of them. Seemingly overwhelmed by the multitude of her playthings, she sometimes goes from toy to toy without spending time on any one of them. She appears to look to toys for amusement and distraction, not imaginative inspiration. It is probably a generational issue, but I find it hard to convince her parents that, when it comes to toys, less is more. Only when a child spends time with a particular toy can she weave it into a story tapestry of her own invention.

The abundance of toys has helped produce a generational shift suggested by my personal experience. In the past it was often the grandparents who spoiled their grandchildren with too many gifts and it was the parents who worried about the rules. I can't be the only grandparent who is dazzled by a visit to FAO Schwarz or Toys R Us. There are so many toys, and so many that I can't recognize, identify with, or feel comfortable buying. When my granddaughters were very young, it was easy. We chose blocks or a sand box or wooden puzzles. Thanks to the automation of so many toys for older children, it gets harder to choose toys that encourage fantasy and imagination.

The abundance and variety of toys reflect, in addition to their availability and low cost, the attitude that contemporary parents have toward toys. Could generous toy giving be an expression of parental guilt for not spending more time with their children? A recent survey shows just the opposite, and this despite the fact that today there are more two-parent working families and single-parent families than in the past. According to a survey conducted at the University of Michigan by S. L. Hofferth, mothers spent 25.05 hours a week with their children in 1987 but 30.89 hours with them in 1997. For fathers, the figures were 18.51 and 22.73, respectively.[1]

Guilt, then, is not the most likely explanation for the profusion of toys given to contemporary children. Childhood has become commercialized as children are viewed as a niche market. Toy manufacturers spend millions each year researching the likes and dislikes of young consumers and spend similar sums on advertising.[2] They target children directly and encourage them to pester their parents (the so-called nag factor) to buy what they see advertised and promoted. Advertisers create needs for toys, and parents give in because they don't want their child to be the only one without the popular plaything. Fad toy production has multiplied in recent years as spin-offs of movie and TV characters. Purchasing fad toys has always been one of the ways parents try to ensure that their children do not feel different or left out.

An unintended consequence of using toys to promote social acceptance and positive self-esteem is that it encourages conformity. Children come to see toys as vehicles of social acceptance rather than launching pads to imagination and fantasy. In addition, toys are used as bragging points against children whose parents are less forthcoming. This is not a new phenomenon. I recall pestering my mother to buy a certain cereal so I could collect the box tops. With six box tops and a nickel I could get a Captain Midnight code ring and book. But my mother did not buy us that cereal and a nickel was a lot of money. I kept pestering her and complaining about not having what my friends had. Finally, exasperated with my nagging and having housework and other children to deal with, my mother said firmly and conclusively, "Who cares what you want?" My mother cared about what we needed but didn't worry about what we wanted. This is one of my fondest memories of my mother and, even though I didn't appreciate it at the time, it has guided me in my own child rearing. In the World War II era, of course, peer acceptance and self-esteem did not loom as large as they do today. Given the media hype over contemporary toys and parental concern with protecting their children's presumably fragile egos, the distinction between what children need and what they want is much harder to make.

All-the-Time Toys

Anyone who lives with children is no stranger to Toyland. You don't need to make a trip to a toy store anymore. Toyland is with us wherever we go. Supermarkets, pharmacies, restaurants, museums, zoos, and even twenty-four-hour convenience stores have toys for sale. "Forget it," you may say to your child, "I'm not buying you any toys today." Or, "Put it back, you just got a toy. You don't need that!"

Yet the toys on the shelves seem to trigger an endless round of "Buy me's" all the same.[3]

Having too many toys and having them all the time, children find it difficult to become attached to toys and select the ones that stimulate their fantasy and imagination. Battery-operated toys are attention getting and use up children's time but are of little or no developmental value. Ironically the sheer abundance, variety, and omnipresence of toys make it harder for children to engage in truly imaginative play with them.

Now that children receive toys all year around, they are no longer as special or as precious as they once were. A child who is given a toy at Christmas and knows that another one is not forthcoming till his next birthday will invest emotionally in that toy and use it as a healthy prop for creating personal fantasies. In addition, toys purchased for a birthday or Christmas are often thoughtful in the sense that parents choose something in keeping with the child's talents and interests. But when toys are purchased because they are tied in to a movie, television program, or book, they don't have any personal meaning or significance. That is another reason why toys purchased continuously fail to engage children's creative fantasy.

In a time when toys were few and far between, they gave flight to a child's imagination. A personal example may help make the point. When we went to visit my wife's niece over the holidays, we didn't expect a two-year-old cousin to be there. We had no present for her. My wife found a bar of lavender soap that we were going to use as a stocking stuffer. She wrapped it and tied it with a pretty bow. When StellaBlue opened the package, her eyes widened and she shouted in delight. Her own bar of soap! She clung to it with great happiness and I could tell that for her, it was bar of gold, a secret treasure, a perfumed soap fit for a princess like her. For StellaBlue, the bar of soap was special and precious because it was so different, and so much more personal, than the other gifts she usually got at the holidays. Children are robbed of that wonderful joy and flights of fancy when toys are no longer special.

Whimsy and imagination are often stimulated by the simplest things, as in the case of StellaBlue. This imaginative activity is the basis of creativity in the arts and sciences. In the past children created their own playthings out of rolling pins, pie and muffin tins, and even Kleenex boxes. Yet children today, thanks in part to receiving toys regularly, seem not to have the opportunity to develop these potentials. Psychiatrist Alvin Rosenfeld recounts the following anecdote:

I have observed the steady decline of play over the past 30 years, but even I was astonished by a recent call from a counselor at an elementary school nearby. She had been talking with a first grade class and used the word imagination. The children stared blankly at her, she explained the meaning, but the children continued to look puzzled. She gave an example from her own childhood when she loved to play Wonder Woman. She would put on a cape, she said, and run down the hill near her home with her arms outstretched, pretending to be aloft. "That's imagination when you pretend to be someone you're not," she explained to the children.

"But we don't know how to do that," said one child and all the others nodded in agreement. Not one child in the first grade seemed to know what imagination was.[4]

To be sure, children are still drawn to toys that nourish their need for imaginative play, and many children still become attached to their toys and build a fantasy life around them. This explains the longevity of some toys and the disappearance of others.

Sensational Toys

Young children are heavily oriented to the senses. Famed Italian educator Maria Montessori called early childhood the *sensitive period*.[5] She realized that young children take comfort and pleasure in the feel of wood, cotton or wool, and metal. She employed cotton yarns dyed with basic colors to stimulate children's visual sense. Such sensory stimulation benefits older children as well. Montessori, of course, wrote before the introduction of plastic and computerized toys. She would probably say that such toys do not give children the rich sensory experience afforded by the materials she employed. Certainly artificial materials are part of our contemporary world. But if children are first exposed to toys made of natural materials, they will have a healthy standard by which to judge synthetics.

Natural materials like cotton and wool (assuming you are not allergic) elicit a sense of a comfort and warmth that synthetics do not. Touch is a powerful sensory experience. Famed psychologist Harry Harlow found that infant monkeys preferred a soft terry cloth "mother" that did not provide milk to a hard wire "mother" that did.[6] Other research demonstrates that for infants, cuddling and fondling by caregivers is critical to their healthy development; contact with human skin is a soothing sensory experience. We should not underestimate the comforting and stress-reducing qualities of natural materials, particularly for young children.

Microchip Toys

Toys containing embedded computer chips have also affected what children learn from toy play. Spring-wound and battery-operated toys were limited in what they could do, but embedded computer chips have vastly increased the range of activities performed by toys. And the number of these toys is increasing at an astonishing rate:

> All kinds of toys are going high tech—industry analysts estimate that at least 75 percent of toys debuting this year will have a mini-chip. Even those toys that have survived because of their open-endedness are being transformed by the introduction of microchips. . .
>
> A new battery-powered Etch A Sketch will rely on digital electronics for a speedy interpretation of each knob twist. It is designed, its makers say, to transmit data along a wire plugged into a television set that will display every line and detail in real time, with accompanying sounds and real color. It will cost $20.00, twice the price of the original Etch A Sketch.[7]

The electronic version of Etch A Sketch makes the whole experience more artificial than the analog version. The analog version allowed children to see the physical results of their actions on the board, and they could adjust their actions accordingly. When a child sees what he is drawing on a TV screen, it is a step removed from his real actions. The child operating the original Etch A Sketch could see how his actions produced the lines, but the electronic version leaves him with little or no understanding of how his actions are translated into an electronic image. The electronic version takes away the child's sense of control over what he is doing and is not likely to be as popular as the original.

The toy industry is promoting toys with embedded computers in an attempt to stem falling sales attributable to high-tech products designed for adults but appropriated by children. School-age children can now be seen with $300 iPods, expensive cell phones, or portable DVD players. Toy makers describe this phenomenon as "age compression." Children today are regarded as more sophisticated than children of earlier generations, and toy makers like Hasbro, Fisher-Price, and others are coming out with high-tech toys that parents can afford.[8]

This appropriation and transformation of adult artifacts into child playthings and pastimes is nothing new, of course, and is a familiar pattern. "In the fourteenth century, Jacks were mechanical wooden figures that struck bells in Church Towers, by the sixteenth century these objects of communal pleasure were miniaturized as string pulled 'jumping jacks' and were sold widely as toys in central Europe. Toy balloons were given to children when French aristocrats, celebrating the first hot air balloon's ascension, grew tired of them."[9] Boys have always created their own versions of the tools and weapons used by the men in their society. Native American boys made their own bows and arrows, toy spears, and stone hammers. In colonial times toys included a looking glass, a spying glass, a drum, a doll, and a watch. Centuries later, with the introduction of the automobile, boys constructed their own version—soapbox cars. Children also appropriated adult literature. Novels like *Gulliver's Travels*, *Robinson Crusoe*, and *Alice in Wonderland* were allegories written for adults but were adopted by children because they were such good stories.

Clearly there is nothing novel about children taking over adult playthings and amusements. But the speed of downsizing and the high level of technology that is incorporated into these child-friendly electronic gadgets is new. The complexity of electronic technology changes the child's intellectual engagement with these toys. The mechanics of soapbox cars and windup toys are easy for children to understand. Toys with embedded microcontrollers, in contrast, work as if by magic. Four- to eight-year-old children cannot understand the electronics behind the CoolP3, an MP3 player for preschoolers, or the Blueberry, a handheld personal planner for preteens. Does this really make a difference? I believe it does. For one thing, a child who is curious about how a jumping jack or windup toy works can figure it out. But there is no way a young child is going to understand the electronics of CoolP3 or Blueberry. It is at least possible that children's inability to figure out how their playthings work can dampen their scientific curiosity.

Even young children may be amazingly adept in using technology. But the ability to use something well doesn't necessarily require an understanding of how it works. It is the difference between a typewriter and a computer. You can type on a computer keyboard with the same facility as a typewriter. But when a typewriter doesn't work you can usually figure out what is wrong. But if your computer suddenly crashes, it is hard to know what is going on. For adults this is frustrating enough, but for children it must be even more so. We are living in a high-tech world and children must learn to use technology. But there is a time for everything. Children's curiosity should still be encouraged and supported through the provision of toys that can satisfy their curiosity about how things work.

There is another possibly negative consequence of automated toys that we need to consider: our increasingly technological, automated society is taking us farther away from the natural world. In our high-tech, superfast world, we may deny our biological nature and begin to think of ourselves in mechanical terms and microchip time. The popularity of cosmetic surgery, particularly for adolescents, is but one expression of this tendency to think of ourselves in nonhuman terms.

Efforts to deny or conceal aging are another example. This mode of thinking comes out in many different ways. One of the preschoolers in our Children's School at Tufts University was on the potty chair and not having much success. After a few moments he told his teacher, "I guess I need new batteries." Nonetheless, we have to accept the fact that we are an animal species and still operate on a biological time clock. Efforts to address emotional issues, physical limitations, and aging are hampered when we think of ourselves in mechanical rather than human terms.

Changes in the Social Benefits of Toy Play

Like it or not, in every society girls play with baby dolls as props to their imagination and fantasy. Such play anticipates at least one potential aspect of their adult roles. Likewise, boys all over the world play with toy replicas of the tools and weapons used by the men of their society. In this way children nourish their capacity for make-believe and also gain a sense of comfort with, and mastery over, grown-up skills. In many parts of the world children's toy play continues to serve both as a stimulus for imagination and a means of socialization into the adult culture. Contemporary toys continue to socialize children as they did in the past. But today, toys serve to instill the psychology of consumerism as much or more than they serve the inculcation of manners, morals, and social roles.

The socializing function that toys played in the past is described by sociologist Gary Cross:

[Post–Civil War] Manufacturers had not yet discovered the possibilities of selling personalities and imagination. Even if they had, few late-nineteenth-century parents would not have approved of such toys. Toymakers sold objects whose purpose was conventional and well understood by the parents who purchased them. They were to be used by children to imitate adult roles and *not* to reenact the fantasy lives of heroes who had little or nothing to do with their own worlds. The character of toys and the advertising clearly reflected the fact that adults, not children, decided what toys should be purchased. Advertising copy stressed durability and educational value. The pull, or mechanical, toy was to distract the irritable or troublesome child. The mechanical bank, a big seller in the 1870s and 1880s, pleased adults because it taught children the valuable lesson of thrift while it entertained them.[10]

The socialization function of toys changed dramatically amid the social upheavals of mid-twentieth-century America. The Vietnam War, the civil rights movement, the women's movement, and the war on poverty helped spread a new egalitarian ethos in society at large. The Pill, the sexual revolution, and no-fault divorce laws changed the sentiments and values of the family. Premarital sex, cohabitation, and divorce became socially acceptable. These attitudinal and value shifts brought about tectonic changes in child rearing and in the conception of the child. For the first time in our history, placing infants and young children in the care of nonparental caregivers (once reserved for the wealthy) became socially acceptable at all social classes. Children who were once regarded as innocent and in need of adult guidance and protection came to be seen as competent—ready and able to deal with all of life's vicissitudes.

The concept of childhood competence is not based on groundbreaking research about the nature of the child. Rather, it has taken hold thanks to social changes that severely limit parents' ability to protect their children. For one thing, given the pervasiveness of television in the home, parents can no longer control the information flow to their children. It is impossible for them to know what will be shown on a television newscast. In the same way, new attitudes about divorce ensure that many parents will split; currently about 50 percent of marriages end in divorce. In addition, the large number of two-income and single-parent homes means that children are often on their own or under nonparental care. Under these changed social circumstances parents have to believe (to retain their sanity) that their children are competent to deal with the early-twenty-first-century social reality. Certainly children were more competent than they were credited with being during the first half of the twentieth century. But they are less competent than we give them credit for today.

An unintended consequence of the new conception of childhood competence is that industry now regards children as a niche market. Many children have money of their own to spend, and advertisers target them directly. They know that brand loyalties, when established early, are remarkably long-lived. So merchandisers go out of their way to get even young children into designer clothes and familiarize them with product logos. Last but not least, children often influence how parents spend their money. They help decide which breakfast food, snacks, and sweets parents purchase. As they get older they may also have a say in which restaurant a family goes to, what car it drives, and where the family vacations.

Given these considerations, those who market toys to children are more interested in creating demand for their products than in meeting children's socialization needs. While some traditional socialization toys continue to be manufactured and marketed—toy trucks, dolls, and dollhouses—many others have little or no personal or socialization value. Robo pets and battery-operated cars and boats don't leave much to the imagination.

There is an interesting parallel between the concept of women as consumers created at the beginning of the twentieth century and children as consumers created in the twenty-first century. During the nineteenth century, the growth of industrialization separated the workplace from the home. Women who had moved from the farm to the city were encouraged to give up their handicraft culture such as needlepoint, quilting, and making preserves. The home economics movement promoted the idea that women needed to be trained to use the new technology of homemaking. Its fictional spokesperson, Betty Crocker, derided the handicraft culture as old-fashioned. "Why," Betty Crocker asked, "should you waste your precious time doing needlepoint or quilting, when you can buy these products ready made at your Sears?" Likewise, she asked, "Why do you need to make preserves when you can buy them at your grocery store? What you need to learn is how to be a modern smart shopper." Thanks to the home economics movement, an imposed consumer culture replaced a self-created handicraft culture.[11]

Like women at the beginning of the twentieth century, children in the twenty-first have been transformed from net producers of their own toy and play culture to net consumers of a play culture imposed by adults. To be sure, some of the toys, games, and entertainments that children enjoy today continue their function of socializing children into the adult world. Like it or not, this socialization is organized along sexist lines. Miniature cars, boats, and airplanes are marketed for boys. Dolls, dollhouses, and child-size household appliances are marketed to girls. Some long-lived unisex games, such as Monopoly, checkers, and chess, as well as card games, are still with us.

Despite the proliferation of toys, contemporary children spend much less time with toys and games than did children of earlier generations. Most of their time is taken up with preprogrammed computer toys and games that may have little if any socialization value other than instilling the need for more of the same. And such play takes away from physical exercise as well. According to studies by the National Sporting Goods Association and American Sports Data (a research firm), on a typical day, a child is six times more likely to play a computer game than ride a bike.[12]

The transformation of toys into vehicles for indoctrinating children in the psychology of consumerism can be seen in each of the three major categories of socialization toys: character toys, skill toys, and educational toys. These toys once served to socialize children into social roles, vocations, and academic tool skills. Today they are more likely to encourage brand loyalties, fashion consciousness, and groupthink.

Character Toys

Character toys originated in children's need for adult role models to help them fashion their sense of self. In the past, character toys reflected the attitudes and values of the larger adult society. Abe Lincoln and Florence Nightingale were popular and good examples of the distant past. Playing with such dolls purportedly helped children learn the positive values and traits associated with those characters. However, character toys took a different turn with the introduction of mass-produced toys and new methods of mass communication. Mickey Mouse came first and can be appreciated as a transition figure. He was fantastical but also represented positive values of friendship, kindness, and generosity. He was followed by a new genre of character toys, the superheroes. Superman, Spiderman, and Batman were positive in that they were human, lived in the real world, and represented the forces of good as opposed to the forces of evil.

The socializing function of character toys took a new turn after the 1970s, once children came to be seen as consumers. Toy manufacturers and advertisers conducted extensive research on children's preferences and learned that "personality promotes loyalty."[13] This means that children easily recognize and identify with characters and story lines associated with them. When toy manufacturers produce a character that is attractive to children, they can sell all the accessories associated with it too, thus creating a so-called consumption net.[14] Barbie, G.I. Joe, and Pokemon make their associated products immediately recognizable and memorable. The point is that these characters are not created to instill positive attitudes and values but to imprint children with a brand name. Even preschoolers now talk about their Disney princess or Bratz dolls.

A good example of the transformation of a relatively child-centered character doll into a consumption net doll is Barbie. Introduced in 1959, Barbie was one of the first character toys embellished with personality. She was a best-seller for Mattel for twenty years and found a place in the toy chest of millions of girls. Barbie already reflected the new (to some parents troubling) trend in toys because she was oriented to fashion rather than homemaking. Even her form evoked controversy: the doll's measurements translated into an unattainable thirty-nine-inch bust, twenty-one-inch waist, and thirty-three-inch hips.

As a fashion plate, Barbie went through about one hundred new outfits each year. She had outfits designed by Yves St. Laurent, Christian Dior, Valentino, Perry Ellis, Oscar de la Renta, and Bob Mackie. Since 1959, over 105 million yards of cloth have been used to make Barbie's clothes. Mattel is thus a huge consumer of fabric and is also America's fourth largest maker of "women's" clothes. But Barbie is not one of the world's most popular toys because of her face, figure, and stylish clothing. She also models a number of careers, including teacher, astronaut, veterinarian, soldier, singer, flight attendant, and model. She keeps up with the latest technology and got her first computer in 1980.[15]

Barbie was introduced before the consumption net existed and was marketed as a stand-alone toy that captured girls' fascination with clothing, hairstyles, and makeup as well as nontraditional careers. She was still a role model in these respects. Initially Barbie was marketed without a TV program and without licensing agreements to sell related products. Barbie's sales began falling in 1985, and the old strategy of updating her with new accessories and advertising campaigns was not helping. In 1986 Barbie was seriously challenged for the first time by Hasbro's Jem.

Consistent with the notion of a consumption net, toy manufacturers decided to introduce Jem with a television program featuring Japanese animation and a comprehensive license-oriented marketing plan. The market for Jem was four- to nine-year-olds.

Girls were attracted to the animation. In addition to the program, Jem was spot-marketed on many channels and at many times. Accessories, like T-shirts and tape recorders, and all of the goods associated with the character were published in a catalog. Carefully thought out narratives went along with the accessories. Jem is a good example of how character toys are used to instill the consumer mentality.

Barbie fought back. In 1987 Mattel decided to give Barbie a television program and her own rock band to compete with Jem's animation. But these plans went counter to the wishes of Ruth and Elliot Handler, who created Barbie and didn't want her personality to be overcommercialized. Ruth Handler said, "Each little girl has her own dreams about who Barbie is. . . . If you give her a specific personality, it would mean that little girls will lose their ability to project whatever personalities they want on Barbie."[16] But the new managers at Mattel, the company founded by the Handlers, disagreed. They were convinced that fantasies based on research and designed and scripted by marketers would sell more Barbie dolls than leaving the toy to girls' own imaginations. Barbie was reborn and the changes stimulated a healthy growth in the fashion doll industry. Other character toys, such as Hasbro's G.I. Joe, had a similar history. Such character toys are now geared mainly to selling associated products in the consumption net and reinforcing brand loyalties.

Aware that some parents may object to the blatant consumerism of Barbie and G.I. Joe, another company introduced the American Girl Collection. In contrast to character toys such as Barbie and G.I. Joe that have questionable social significance, the American Girl dolls have real historical relevance. They are dressed in clothing appropriate to the historical period the doll represents. However, the high price of these dolls and their associated books shows that the American Girl dolls reflect a clever (some might say cynical) marketing ploy aimed at upscale parents who want something more exclusive than Barbie. They are a thinly disguised vehicle for appealing to more affluent parents. With all of today's character toys, what sells takes precedence over what might be good for children.

Skill Toys

In general, skill toys require children to learn one or more skills. They are the most universal playthings and probably have the longest history. In every era boys play with miniature tools and weapons used by men while girls play with miniature implements used by women. The same is true today. As we moved from a farming society to an industrial society, skill toys changed accordingly. Inasmuch as skill toys were, and continue to be, designed to socialize children into prescribed sex roles, we will consider the toys for boys and girls separately.

Skill Toys for Boys.   During the first half of the twentieth century, miniature versions of new inventions such as the electric motor, the internal combustion engine, the airplane, the radio, photographic film, and the telephone became available to boys. These skill toys included kits for making crystal radios, model airplanes, model electric trains, and child-size cameras. Small electric motors made it possible to bring machine tools into the home, and this was the start of the "do it yourself" home improvement movement. Boys were encouraged to begin learning about this brave new world with woodworking, chemistry, woodburning, and lead soldier modeling kits. They also played with toy cars, boats, and airplanes, some with battery-operated motors.

Today toys with embedded computers have supplanted skill toys. It is impossible for children to build their own computers, CD players, or video cameras. The few skill toys that remain, such as Legos, are limited to teaching construction and mechanical skills. Attempts to construct computer skill toys that children can use to create their own programs have not been successful. Computer scientist Seymour Papert's Logo program for teaching children programming skills is perhaps the best known.[17] Introduced more than two decades ago, it has yet to be widely implemented. Indeed, it is hard to imagine a kit that children could use to build a computer or write a computer program from scratch. Children can learn computer skills without ever understanding how the computer works. In contrast, a boy who built a crystal radio set knew how it operated as well as how to use it.

Skill Toys for Girls.   Skill toys for girls have a similar history. During the first half of the twentieth century girls were given miniatures of new household appliances such as refrigerators, stoves, washing and sewing machines. Toy typewriters were also available. It was a time of strict gender role definition, and these toys were meant to instill homemaker attitudes, values, and skills. Baby dolls, carriages, and dollhouses were also common. Girls were also given toy irons for pressing clothing and toy bowls and mixers for making cookies and puddings. The reason for calling these various implements toys is that they left room for the child to imagine herself as a grown-up performing these activities as an adult.

The changes in society and the advent of computer and microchip technology have also done away with many of these skill toys for girls. As women have expanded their educational and occupational horizons, traditional roles have broken down. Skill toys for girls are no longer limited to those related to housekeeping and child care. Girls now spend as much time on computers as boys, and computer, Internet, and cell phone use are the unisex skills of the new millennium. Girls probably use these skills more for social interaction (instant messaging), whereas boys are more likely to use them for game playing. Yet the new computer skills don't really prepare children for the more mundane and practical skills of everyday life. Many young people today do not learn practical homemaking skills until they are on their own.

This is as true for occupational skills as it is for homemaking ones. The need for hands-on play is now recognized in higher education. In the school of architecture at Stanford University, students are required to play with erector sets as part of the curriculum. Too few students have had actual experience in building real things, which is essential before they begin designing them. The dean of the school of engineering at Iowa State University made a similar point to me when I visited. "Do you know who make the best engineers?" he asked, and then answered his own question: "Those young men and women who grew up on the farm and had firsthand experience with machinery." Those young people gain a practical understanding of how machines work, what they can and cannot do.

A personal example may highlight this point. My father was a master machinist in a plant that made automobile parts. I still recall the many evenings when he would come home frustrated and angry. Again and again he was given blueprints drawn up by college trained engineers. The problem was that the parts they drew on paper, while beautiful, could not be machined. My father, who was not college trained, had to redesign the parts so that they could be turned on a lathe or a milling machine. Engineers were designing parts without having any idea of how these parts were actually tooled in the machine shop.

To be sure, the world is much more automated than it was in my father's day. Many craft skills like running milling or linotype machines have been taken over by computers. But there is still a place for craftsmanship and there always will be. Indeed, many skills that were once lost are now coming back as handicrafts and arts. Handmade pottery, weaving, metal, and glass are now in high demand. As I suggested earlier, abundance can breed contempt. When machine-made goods are in such abundance, hand-crafted goods take on a new value and significance. Equally important, craft skills reunite us with the real world. They also reunite play, love, and work. For all of these reasons, true skill toys should still find a place in the contemporary child's tool chest.

Educational Toys

One legacy of our Puritan heritage is a lingering ambivalence toward child play. On the one hand, our work ethic makes us regard play as slothful and a waste of time. This attitude has been reinforced by contemporary changes in society. In today's high-tech society education is the only way to avoid menial occupations. As a result the competition is intense as parents compete to get their children into the top schools (including nursery schools). On the other hand, we believe that play is a healthy pastime for children. Many of us recall growing up with the freedom to play with our friends without many of the constraints placed on contemporary young people.

The concept of the educational toy helps resolve this contradiction between the belief that play is wasteful and the conviction that it is healthy. Educational toys are nothing new; many early toy makers claimed that their toys taught children basic skills and values. Prior to World War II, educational toys were designed to teach character and moral values. Today educational toys are narrowly conceived and designed to teach academic skills.

Most contemporary educational toys are created for preschool children, fueled by a widespread belief that education is a race and the earlier you start the better. The fastest-growing software for children is so-called lapware for infants from six months to two years. The infant sits on the parent's lap, looks at the computer screen, and interacts with it by pushing a mushroom-shaped mouse. Programs like Baby Wow purport to teach children their colors, shapes, and so on. A number of CDs are also available for infants, including the Baby Einstein series. I watched Baby Einstein and Baby Newton with my granddaughter Heather, who was eighteen months old at the time. She seemed to listen to the music but seldom watched the moving geometric forms on the screen. I wasn't sure what they were supposed to teach her.

For three- to five-year-old children there are even more educational toys. By far the largest producer and merchandiser of educational material for children is the LeapFrog company. The motto of this firm is "Learn something new every day." The games in LeapFrog's arsenal of learning toys are claimed to do everything from raising a child's self-esteem to stimulating brain growth. But there is little research that supports these claims.[18]

Professionals disagree as to the value of these early stimulation and education programs. Some argue that the brain is growing rapidly during this period and consequently stimulation is necessary to take advantage of this growth. Those who argue against this position point out that it is not the number of neurons in the brain that is important but rather the complexity of their connections. Indeed, a lot of synaptic pruning goes on in the early years so that older children have fewer neurons but more connections than preschoolers. At this point there is little clear evidence for either position.

What is clear is that these educational toys for young children are another example of how toys have become part of the consumer culture. Parents are encouraged to buy such toys to give their children an educational edge. And there is a subtle message that parents who do not buy these educational toys for their children are really not doing a good job as parents. What I find troubling about these products is that they are designed and marketed more for their appeal to parents than for what is really in the best interests of the child. In the past, toy manufacturers tried to make toys that reflected parental beliefs and values. Today they create toys that speak to parental fears and anxieties.

Toys are but one facet of the changing world of play. Screen-based play is another part of this transformation of the child's world. It is a new form of play ushered in by the advent of electronic media. Because it is so new and is changing so rapidly, its effects are difficult to evaluate. Screen play has created many new challenges for parents that we will review in the next chapter.

three

Screen Play and Iconic Literacy

Most Americans, including children and adolescents, spend an increasing number of hours each day in front of TV, computer, movie, BlackBerry, and cell phone screens. Screens have transformed the way both adults and children live. From the perspective of this book, screens have contributed dramatically to the changing world of children's play. Much of the time children once spent playing outdoors is now occupied by sedentary screen play. Screens are part of our environment and we have to adapt to them. The question for us as parents is, When, how much, and at what pace should we introduce children to the many faces of electronic media? There is no simple answer to this question, and professionals disagree about what constitutes a healthy screen diet for young people. In this chapter I provide some guidance on these questions, taking into account both individual differences among children and the age appropriateness of the various media being marketed to young people.

Electronic Media

When *Jurassic Park* was released, a *Boston Globe* reporter invited me to join her and a couple of other professionals to attend a matinee screening of the film. She was going to do a piece on *Jurassic Park* and wanted to incorporate our evaluations of the film and the audience reactions into her article. She chose the matinee to ensure that there would be a large number of children to observe. For me, the children were much more interesting than the film. When the scary parts came on, when the dinosaurs were attacking, some of the children watched eagerly, some laughed and giggled, and still others hid their faces. Many children liked this scary film, while others clearly did not. As far as I could tell it was not a matter of age or sex. There were younger children who liked the film and older children who did not. And from what I could see, there were as many girls as boys enjoying the movie.

The range of children's reactions to *Jurassic Park* underlines the complexity of our adaptation to the multiple screen worlds of contemporary life. We are individuals, and how we respond to screen content is at least partly determined by our personality traits, attitudes, and values. The same movie can turn some children on and others off. This is not a new phenomenon. None of us like exactly the same films as our parents, friends, or even spouses. But when it comes to our children and movies, television, or computer games, we tend to think of them as having the same impact on all young people. This one-sided way of looking at contemporary screen media is typical of what happens to all communication technologies when they are new. Comic books, dime novels, radio, movies, television, and rock and roll were all initially accused of corrupting youth.

Of course movies, television, and computer games can be harmful to young people. But the relation between the child and screen media is a multifaceted interaction that can't be reduced to a simple cause-and-effect connection. This is where my theory of play can help. To leave a lasting impression, the media have to give the viewer a chance to take some initiative (play), to be emotionally involved (love), and to learn something about the world (work). We tend to focus on the emotions that the screen media arouse in children or the negative values or attitudes they may take away from it. At the same time, we tend to pay less heed to whether or not the child is actively engaged with the program. Yet it is the extent of the child's active participation as a viewer that determines the media's impact.

This is where literary scholar and media interpreter Marshall McLuhan went astray. McLuhan was one of the first of the media mavens and wrote about the media from a broad social-historical perspective. He believed that the electronic media are bringing about a fundamental change in our way of thinking similar to the one generated by the introduction of print media. It is generally accepted today that people in preliterate, oral cultures thought differently than do people in literate societies.[1] Before writing was invented, people could only store information by memorizing it and passing it on through oral tradition. Memorization was thus a major tool of preliterate thought. The techniques of rhythm, rhyme, and repetition were the primary aids to memorization. In preliterate societies, concepts and ideas were necessarily concrete and often tied to pictorial representations, or icons. With the introduction of writing, people no longer had to rely on memory or icons to retain information. Print freed the literate world from the concreteness of the preliterate world and made abstract thought possible.

McLuhan argued forcibly that the "medium is the message," by which he meant that the form of communication—oral, print, or electronic—was more important than the content conveyed.[2] While this was certainly the case for the transition from oral to print culture, it has not yet been proven to be the case for electronic media, at least not in the way McLuhan envisioned it. Rather, what we are seeing, particularly since the advent of computers, is not so much a new way of thinking as a new form of literacy—*iconic* literacy. In many respects, the new media have reintroduced us to the rich world of pictorial icons and memorization that dominated the preliterate world. An icon is more than a picture or drawing because it is functional and is used to perform some task. You just have to look at your computer screen desktop, your cell phone, your BlackBerry, or any computer game to recognize the extent to which icons permeate our world and our thinking. In contrast to adults, who have to struggle to remember what all these icons mean and do, young children are preliterate and have an intuitive grasp of, and memory for, icons. This intuitive iconic literacy may be one of the reasons children take so readily to electronic media. Whether this form of literacy supports, inhibits, or has no effect on print literacy is yet to be determined.

Media: Hot and Cold

Nevertheless, McLuhan made many valuable contributions to our understanding of media. One of his most powerful insights was the idea that media and media content can be described on a continuum from hot to cool.

> Any hot medium allows of less participation than a cool one. As a lecture allows for less participation than a seminar, and a book for less than dialogue. . . . High definition or intensity engenders specialization and fragmentation in living as in entertainment, which explains why any intense experience must be "forgotten" or "censored" and reduced to a very cool state before it can "learned" or assimilated.[3]

With respect to content, high-definition, high-intensity, "hot" content is more fully engaging but demands less viewer participation than does low-definition, low-intensity, "cool" content. (McLuhan used "cool" in the way we use it in slang to suggest someone who is with it but also a bit detached from it.) A photograph is highly defined and intense, whereas a sketch is less defined and less intense. The sketch invites more active participation than does the photograph. This way of looking at media content provides a fresh approach to understanding the relationship between it and viewers. Consider the different reactions to the movie *Jurassic Park*, which is hot in the McLuhan sense of high definition and high intensity. Children who preferred hot media liked it, while those who preferred their media cool did not.

Assessing Media Impact

Accordingly, when we want to assess the impact of screen media (or any media) on children, we have to take several factors into account. First there is the matter of content. It is fairly easy to decide whether a movie, TV program, or computer game is hot or cool in McLuhan's sense. Presentations that are stimulating, visually arresting, and passivity inducing are at the hot and end of the spectrum. Presentations that are slow paced, quiet, and visually interesting are on the cool, activity-inducing side of the continuum. For example, a newscast that shows people lying injured and bleeding on stretchers is high intensity and high definition, requiring little viewer participation other than feeling pity. In contrast, a newscast that shows a person who is grief stricken and speechless is more likely to invoke thoughtful sympathy and compassion. Similarly, nudity and explicit sexual language are hot while seductive clothing and seductive language are cool.

That cool media invite more learning than hot was supported by a study which looked at the television viewing of young children from low- to moderate-income families. Two- to three-year-old children who routinely watched cool television programs like *Sesame Street* did better on academic skill measures (e.g., reading readiness and vocabulary) than did children who routinely watched entertainment programs.[4]

A second factor to be considered is the existence of individual differences among viewers. As children's varying responses to *Jurassic Park* suggested, they, no less than adults, differ in their preferences for hot and cool media. When we think about how media messages affect children, we have to consider not only the media content but also individual differences in media responsiveness. If we observe our children while they are watching TV, it is fairly easy to identify what they do and do not like. My guess is that preferences for hot and cool media are probably consistent personality traits. I would expect, for example, that children who enjoyed *Jurassic Park* would be likely to ride the roller coaster, a hot ride, at an amusement park. In contrast, those who didn't like the film would likely enjoy the Ferris wheel, which is a cool ride.

A longitudinal study of the effects of preschool television viewing on adolescent academic achievement gives evidence for the long-term effects of preferential viewing habits.[5] In one study, children were assessed at age five with respect to the amount of time they spent viewing educational (cool), entertaining (hot), and violent (hot) television programs. Preschoolers who spent the majority of their time watching educational programs had different outcomes at adolescence than did those who spent more time watching entertaining or violent programs. Adolescents who preferred cool educational programs as preschoolers earned higher grades, read more books, placed more value on achievement, and showed greater creativity and less aggression than did preschoolers who preferred hot programs.

The results were more consistent for boys than for girls. Girls who frequently viewed violent programs had lower grades as teenagers than did preschool girls who viewed such programs infrequently. Viewing violent programs did not have the same effect on boys. One possible explanation of this finding is that television viewing has greater impact when it conflicts with sex-typed socialization. Girls who went against type in their television viewing also went against type in their behavior. The study controlled for such variables as family background, other categories of preschool viewing, and adolescent media use. These findings also support the view that hot media are less conducive to positive learning than are cool media.

Finally, we need to remain open to the possibility that a child's personal emotional needs and motivations can sometimes transform a program that is intended to be engaging (hot) into a powerful growth experience (cool). This can happen if the viewer becomes emotionally involved in the plot or with the characters. When he was nine, my middle son actively identified with Danny on *The Partridge Family* and often imitated his voice and actions. This identification helped him deal with a number of issues he was having with his brothers. For my other sons, the show was simply entertaining. When I was a child, I listened with my family to the radio program *One Man's Family*. I still remember identifying with a character named Paul, to whom everyone came with their problems. It has always seemed to me that my early identification with that radio character was one of the reasons I chose to be a clinical psychologist. For me, the program was cool in the McLuhan sense. For my older brother, who didn't like the program, it was neither hot nor cool but simply dull and uninteresting.

In short, we have to be cautious before making simple cause-and-effect connections between what children watch on the screen and their actual behavior. It is a highly complex interaction. Perhaps that is why so much of the research on the effects of TV watching is ambiguous. Too often such research is based on overly simplistic assumptions about the one-way effects of media on children. Perhaps that is why the subject of television watching among infants and young children is extremely controversial.

TV for Tots

A recent survey of 1,065 parents assessing the role of electronic media in the lives of infants and preschoolers found that 25 percent of children under two have televisions in their bedrooms. Two-thirds of children under two use some kind of screen media (computer, DVD, television) on a typical day for about two hours. Children under six spend an average of two hours a day with screen media—three times longer than the time they spend reading or being read to.[6]

It is hard to assess the overall impact of this media exposure on infants and young children, whose visual systems are not fully developed. The American Academy of Pediatrics has advised parents against television viewing by children under two. This caution stems at least in part from the fact that the effect of prolonged TV viewing on the immature eye is not clear. Whether we like it or not, of course, infants *are* watching and listening to television and DVDs. The effects are difficult to assess because we can't be sure how much time the child is actually attending to the screen and what he or she may be taking in. An analysis of a few representative TV and DVD offerings for infants and toddlers affords some guidance for the use and value of this material.

Teletubbies

One of the first television shows for infants and young children was *Teletubbies*. Anne Wood, coproducer of the program, describes its purported benefits:

> *Teletubbies* is crafted with the understanding that little children watch television in a radically different way than do older children and grown-ups. The program makes liberal use of repetition, large movement, bright colors, and deliberate pace to nurture the development of imagination, thinking and listening skills. The stories are structured so that the child is able to stay one step ahead of the *Teletubbies* encouraging abilities of prediction and visualization and, most vitally, developing confidence and self-esteem.[7]

These claims for *Teletubbies* are made on the program's website, but there is no evidence to back them up. These unfounded assertions reflect little or no appreciation of well-established facts of child development. For example, imagination requires representational thinking, which only appears toward the end of the second year. Furthermore, self-confidence and self-esteem require a sense of self that the infant has not yet constructed and the child acquires gradually through the preschool years. The "terrible twos" are terrible because the two-year-old is asserting her emerging sense of self by resisting adult authority. Claims for the educational and personal benefits of a media program for infants and toddlers should, at the very least, show respect for what we know about child growth and development.

From the perspective of "hot" and "cool" media, *Teletubbies* is hot because the producers have built in well-known attention-getting (e.g., bright colors) devices. Infants who have a preference for hot media may watch *Teletubbies* but are more likely to be entertained (pacified) than encouraged to engage in active learning. More importantly, watching *Teletubbies* takes away time from the infant's engaging in self-directed and self-initiated learning. Infants and young children spend many hours sleeping, so it is vitally important that they spend most of their waking time actively relating to caregivers and exploring their sensory world through active play.

Baby Einstein

In addition to TV programs for tots, DVDs for this age-group are being produced by a number of companies. The Baby Einstein videos present colorful pictorial parades and animated cartoons accompanied by different musical backgrounds. *Baby Beethoven*, for example, features many of Beethoven's favorite compositions accompanied by colorful animation. There are DVDs featuring composers—*Baby Beethoven*, *Baby Bach*, and *Baby Mozart*. Representing artists are *Baby DaVinci* and *Baby Monet*. Writers are represented by *Baby Shakespeare* and *Baby Wordsworth* and scientists by *Baby Einstein* and *Baby Galileo*. The *Baby Farmer* DVD features a score based on the "Farmer in the

Dell." Unlike *Teletubbies,* the Baby Einstein series has some redeeming features, though there is again no evidence for their short- or long-term benefits. The music is generally well done and the visuals, though sometimes mystifying, are usually not intrusive and are easily ignored. In this sense the Baby Einstein DVDs are cool in comparison to the hot *Teletubbies.*

I watched a few of these DVDs with my granddaughter Heather when she was a year and a half old. We looked at *Baby Mozart, Baby Einstein,* and *Baby Galileo.* Or rather I watched and Heather listened. She was busy putting her favorite teddy in his chair and arranging his room. I knew she was listening, though, because she was moving in time to the music. For Heather, the video was cool in that she used it for her own purposes. She was not fully engaged by the video. This series may serve other functions for other children. At my granddaughter Lily's birthday party, the discussion turned to the Baby Einstein DVD series. Some parents commented on how entranced their children were by one or the other of the Baby Einstein videos. One parent remarked that the music had a quieting effect when her son was upset.

Consequently I am more sanguine about the Baby Einstein series than I am about *Teletubbies.* The long-term benefits of infants listening to classical music is far from being clearly established. Nonetheless listening to classical music probably does no harm and may have a positive quieting effect on little children. This quality of classical music has long been recognized. As playwright William Congreve put it, "Musick has charms to sooth a savage breast." And because many of the visuals are less intrusive than those on *Teletubbies,* children can enjoy the music—as Heather did—and ignore the visuals.

In defense of two-parent working and single-parent families, Baby Einstein videos can be a blessing. A child quietly watching or listening to a video can give parents precious time to get dressed, have breakfast, and do chores. The same is true when working parents get home at night. And because these videos give parents time to do what they need to do, they may also reduce stress and in this way benefit the whole family.

On the other hand, it really troubles me when I see parents bring their children to preschool with the television on in the back of the SUV. Driving in the car together is a perfect time for parent-child interaction, be it talking, singing, or telling stories. Videos should not be used to avoid interaction with our children. Do not buy into the exaggerated benefits touted for some of these programs and videos. Parents who talk, play with, or sing to their young infants or toddlers give them much more than any DVD or television program ever could. The most important stimulus to healthy growth and development for infants and young children is affectionate human interaction.

CDs and Videos for Preschoolers

The number and range of CDs and videos for preschoolers is growing almost as rapidly as those for infants and toddlers. Some of these programs can be helpful if used in moderation. For this age-group animation should outweigh text, and the slower the pace the better.

Leapfrog Products

The Leapfrog Company is one of the largest marketers of learning and play products for children from infancy through adolescence. Leapfrog markets both videos and computer games for young children. A pair of VHS videotapes entitled *The Letter Factory* and the *Talking Words Factory* are typical of their programs for preschoolers. I would not use these videos for children under four, particularly if their languages skills are not well developed. The ad copy for these two programs reads:

The Letter Factory led by wacky professor Quigley has T's and J's jumping on trampolines and K's practicing karate kicks as each new letter in the factory learns its sound. Fun songs will have kids singing letter sounds in time!

The Talking Words Factory Amazing Inventions puts words together and takes them apart to teach reading and language skills.

These two videos employ conventional links of letter sounds with familiar objects and actions and songs in an animated way. While they may be useful to some young children, they may be too hot for other youngsters who would benefit from the cooler, simpler pictorial presentation in books. If your child is skilled enough to play these videos on his own, let him. Children who are allowed to play these videos at their leisure are likely to gain more from them than if we choose when to put them on. If this type of video is too hot for a child, don't force the issue. In all likelihood the child likes cool media and would much rather look at books or be read to.

As with CDs and videos for infants, it is important to use common sense in deciding how much time a preschooler should spend on such materials. Young children have a lot of energy and need time to engage in active play. Watching videos should not infringe on that time. It is the misuse of these products as baby-sitters or substitutes for active play that is harmful.

Computers for Infants, Toddlers, and Preschoolers

The idea that education is a race seems to extend to computer use. Many parents, aided and abetted by those who produce and sell computer programs for young children, believe early computer use will give their children an edge in our increasingly technological society.

Perhaps that explains why the fastest growing software market is so-called lapware, for infants from six months to two years.

Computer Programs for Infants and Toddlers

Lapware programs are designed for the child to sit on the parent's lap and operate a large mouse and/or keyboard that can be operated by a simple touch or push. A couple of the most popular programs are described below.

Jumpstart Baby.   One of the most ambitious programs for infants and young children (9–24 months) is called Jumpstart Baby. The ad copy describes it as follows:

> Wake up babies, cuddly little Teddy has arrived to spend the day. He hopes to entertain with his upbeat activities—typical baby favorites! All the encouragement he needs is a keystroke here and there. So press the key and let the games begin. . . . Above Teddy's crib hangs a mobile. The objects hanging off the mobile represent different activities to try. Each object twirls in turn, and clicking or pressing a key while it twirls causes the associated activity to commence. Baby can choose to dress Teddy—for snow or sand, find his farm animal friends and hear his sounds, sort colored objects on a Color Train, join in a Sing A Long with Teddy's band, connect stars to draw pictures in the sky.

The creators of Jumpstart Baby claim that it has the following educational values:

> Jumpstart Baby offers familiar early learning experience via the computer screen. These favorite games are crucial elements in the

development of critical thinking skills. Although interaction is minimal, it is enough to give the child a sense of control. With adult supervision the child can learn to tap lightly on the keyboard keys and/or click the mouse when the Teddy asks and experience the result of these actions.

The benefits claimed for this program are ridiculous. How can an infant learn critical thinking skills before he has the reasoning tools needed to think critically? An infant who drops a rattle out of the crib and gets the parent to retrieve it experiences a sense of control of his actions. And by repeating the process, the infant clearly demonstrates that he appreciates the result of this action. The infant doesn't need a computer to learn that.

Baby WOW.   Another software product for infants is Baby WOW. The advertisement for Baby WOW reads as follows:

> There's no replacement for your baby's or toddler's discovery of the real world. . . . The computer has many wonderful attributes that make it a valuable tool for parents of young children, such as its ability to deliver high-quality sounds and images while teaching cause-and-effect relationships. Baby WOW 3.0 was created to reward a child's natural curiosity about the computer with an interactive experience based on early development research. Baby WOW speaks 8 languages and lets you add your own pictures. It doesn't replace anything in your child's life. Instead, it creates a new opportunity for you and your child to learn and interact together.

An infant may be curious about a hot stove or brightly colored pills, but she should not be allowed to experiment with them. And in what way does the program speaking eight different languages help a child who is just learning her own language? If parents speak a foreign language, it makes sense for the child to hear it and to learn to speak it. In young children, the major hindrance to learning a foreign language is motivation. Why should an infant learn a language that no one in her environment knows or speaks? Clearly this language offering is thrown in for its parental appeal rather than any practical value for the child. Again, the entire rationale for this program, as for Jumpstart Baby, is to entice parents.

With any of the computer programs for infants and toddlers, we have to ask, *Is this really necessary?* There is no question that computers are now an integral part of our environment. But so too are so are microwaves, cell phones, and automobiles. If we recognize that it takes a certain level of maturity to use an automobile, why is it so hard to appreciate that the same holds true for computers? There is nothing an infant can learn from a computer program that he cannot learn, more easily and more effectively, from a mobile or crib gym.

There are, moreover, real interpersonal risks involved in the use of these programs with infants. If the infant happens to choose a wrong icon, the parent may become upset—and this feeling is immediately communicated to the sensitive infant. Infants have no conception of right or wrong, but they do know when their parents have positive and negative feelings toward them. It can be frightening for an infant not to know what is making her parent upset or angry. Why put infants in this situation for no purpose?

Computer Programs for Preschoolers

After the age of three or so, most children have pretty good language skills and a reasonable amount of motor control. Some exposure to computer programs at this age can be both educational and fun. The programs need to be age appropriate, and the child should not spend too much time with them. We also have to be open to children using computers in ways that we may not expect or anticipate. I was visiting a preschool that had couple of computers loaded with educational computer games. Several boys were standing around a youngster who was at the keyboard. They were talking and commenting on the progress of the game. The teacher came by and, misreading the situation, told the boys to leave the child at the keyboard alone; they had to take turns. What the teacher missed was that the children were using the game as a cooperative social event, not a competitive one. Children may use computers creatively in ways that seem foreign to us. Sometimes we just need to sit back and watch what children in groups do with computers.

We need to be sensitive to individual preferences as well. Individual learning styles and abilities become increasingly important as the child moves into formal education. As we will see in the next section, different programs appeal to different patterns of abilities. A particular child might like some of these programs but not others. If children have the opportunity to choose, they will eventually find the programs that are most suited to their particular talents and strengths. We need to respect these individual differences and not expect a child to like all programs equally well. Finally, for young children, time spent on the computer should be limited to a half hour or so at most.

Computer Games for School-Age Children

After a lecture I gave to parents about computer games taking time away from experiencing the real world, an embarrassed parent came up to me and told me the following story. Early in the spring he and his wife purchased a new SUV that the family planned to take across country on a long summer vacation. It had a TV and VCR in the rear for the children. The trip was going well and the family made a number of interesting side trips. They were really looking forward to reaching the Grand Canyon. It was approaching sunset when they finally arrived at the canyon. The man parked the SUV, and he and his wife walked over to view the glorious sunset over the canyon. When his two sons did not join them, he called out to them and said they were missing something spectacular. The boys shouted back, "We have to finish our game!"

It should be clear by now that I am not opposed to screen play in principle. How to use screen play in a healthy and responsible way is the real issue. It is sad, for example, when these games take precedence over watching a sunset at the Grand Canyon. Computer games have their place but so does the appreciation of nature. The real challenge, particularly of computer games, is ensuring that they do not take priority over other activities. The educational value of computer games is limited unless directly tied up with the school curriculum—as with some simulation games. Since computer games can become addictive, particularly for some children who may use them to avoid social interaction and/or physical activity, parents must set firm limits on the amount of time children spend on these games.

Iconic Literacy

Computer games are perhaps the best illustration of iconic literacy—reading icons to get information and solve problems. To obtain insight into this process and to offer parents guidelines for the use of these games by young children, I decided to play some on my computer. I urge parents to do likewise. It will give you a sense of the difficulty of the game and whether or not it is appropriate for your child. Playing the game can also afford a topic of conversation and joint interaction. There is an almost infinite variety of these games from the shoot-'em-up to the adventure to history, science, and more. I found that the age ranges for these games are generally exaggerated at the low end. I would add at least two years to the lowest age suggested in the advertising.

For this exercise, I chose games that were in the problem-solving domain, just to see what children might be learning from them. I played one war game to get a feel for the genre, but it required rapid visual motor coordination rather than problem solving so I will not present it here. I started with some of the simplest games, purportedly for the youngest children, and worked my way up to games for older school-age children. Icons are prominent in all of these games.

Piglet (Of Winnie the Pooh Fame)

This game is meant for children from three to eight. That in itself is telling, for, as we will see in later chapters, a huge leap in intellectual ability occurs between the ages of four and six. After playing the game, I would recommend it for six- to eight-year-olds. It might be frustrating for younger children because it requires a kind of reasoning they have not yet attained. The version that I played was simple enough from an adult perspective. Piglet walks across the screen on a pair of stilts. Touching the right/left arrow keys on the computer keyboard makes him go backward or forward. Hitting the up/down arrow keys makes him go higher or lower on the long stilts. Piglet is holding a honey pot and drops of honey are falling from the huge tree in the background. The honey is coming down in a random pattern, and the challenge is to get as much honey as you can into the pot. By trial and error, playing the game several times, I found the most successful strategy. If Pooh is lower on the stilts, you have a better chance of catching the honey than if he is higher. By focusing on the top of the screen you have the best chance of positioning Pooh to catch the most honey.

Many computer games, like this one, resemble the autodidactic materials that Maria Montessori created for preschool children.[8] In the Montessori tasks, however, the child deals with only one dimension at a time, like fitting different-size cylinders into their appropriate holes. The Piglet game is much more complex than the Montessori task. You have to deal with at least three variables—

Piglet's height on the stilts, where the honey is coming from, and where Piglet should be positioned. This is far beyond what most three- and four-year-olds can do. Some children might have fun moving Piglet about while others might not want to play at all. For older children it is a cool game and provides practice in problem solving. But the problem-solving skills children learn in this game are not likely to transfer to other problem-solving situations.

Spy Fox

This is a many-layered game that is advertised for four- to eight-year-olds but also for eight years and up. The age range is so wide because the game has higher-level versions too. I think even the simplest version is too hard for most four- and five-year-olds. The beginning versions may be a way to get children (or parents) to buy the more advanced series. These games have an audio track as well as the visuals. The entry-level game I played begins in the passenger compartment of an airliner where Spy Fox is having his dinner. The stewardess, an agent in disguise, gives him his case assignment. In this instance, the owner of a milk factory has been captured and faces death. They are flying over the factory now. Spy Fox leaps out of the plane and lands in the midst of several doors and a wooden walkway. If you aim the mouse arrow at the walkway, Spy Fox goes down it and encounters a steel door. If you touch him with the arrow, he says, "I am going to do something predictable in a moment." (The voice is similar to that of the late Don Adams in the TV series *Get Smart*.) At the bottom of the screen three objects—a toothbrush, a video screen, and three barrels—pop up for a few seconds. If you click on the toothbrush and drag it over to Spy Fox, he uses it and the toothpaste to blow open the steel door.

Inside, the owner of the factory is suspended over a tub of water filled with piranhas. He is suspended by a rope attached to a pulley. In front of the tub is a meter going from red to blue, hot to cold. If you touch the ice cube on the meter, the dial moves toward the cold end. If you keep touching it, the dial moves over completely and the tub freezes over. Then, if you point the arrow at the stairway leading to the pulley, Spy Fox rushes up the stairs and releases the pulley. The factory owner plummets down and lands on the ice but does not crash through. This sets the stage for the next episode.

Like Piglet, this game begins with a lot of trial-and-error learning. For example, there are a variety of objects in the setting that do things if you click on them. A drain pipe drips water if you click on it, and a mouse jumps out of a barrel if you click on it. But these are irrelevant, and you have to learn to focus on the objects where clicking moves the story forward. Eventually, as with Piglet, you hit on strategies that move you along more quickly. Hitting on the ice cube again and again, for example, moves the dial and freezes the tub. You discover this by trial and error, but then you can turn it into a strategy of effective play. Like Piglet, the game is cool and invites playful learning without being totally absorbing. Like many games, it begins with trial and error but leads, with practice, to time-saving strategies.

Like Piglet, however, this game requires coordinating several different variables and performing tasks sequentially. This calls on short-term memory as well as coordination skills. As such it is much too difficult for preschool children. Icons are prominent in this game and I wonder whether they may facilitate learning for younger children. For me they were stumbling blocks. It would be interesting for a researcher to see if the icons enable children to succeed at this game at an earlier age than their level of mental development would predict. If your child does succeed with such games at an early age, iconic literacy may be at work.

After conquering Spy Fox, I felt empowered to tackle a more complex game.

Professor Fizzwizzle

This puzzle game does not recommend specific ages but has four levels of complexity from child to advanced. Even the first levels are too difficult for preschool children. The story line is that brilliant Professor Fizzwizzle created a number of robots to do household chores, like making the beds, doing the laundry, and washing the dishes. Working late one evening, Professor Fizzwizzle forgot to turn off the robots and they went haywire and are now trying to do him in. His task is to escape the robots before they destroy him. You can play the game on a PC using both the mouse and keyboard arrows. Essentially the game presents the player with a series of increasingly complex mazes. These consist of several different tiers made of different substances like ice, grass, and sand. Obstacles to be overcome are barrels, crates, gates, and dropoffs. There are ladders that go from one tier to another, but the ladders sometimes do not go all the way up or down to the next tier. There are also colored buttons that open like colored gates when depressed.

At the first level, Professor Fizzwizzle appears on a high tier and you have to use the mouse to take him down the ladder and across the grass to reach his safety cubicle. At the next level you have to move a crate on top of a button to open a gate that will let the professor reach safety. The higher levels of difficulty include many more complicated steps. For example, in order to fill a gap in the ground so he can get to his cubicle, the professor has to roll a barrel close to a ladder, climb the ladder to get on the barrel, and roll the barrel into the gap so he can cross. For this game, the best strategy is to study the whole scene and try to figure out the steps in your head before you start moving the professor.

I had a lot of trouble with the higher levels of this game, since I don't have a good spatial sense and get lost easily. For example, I can be in a hotel room for several nights and still not remember whether to turn right or left to get to the elevator.

This is a game for people who have good visual and spatial abilities, and good visual memory. In some ways, it requires the same kind of skills as playing chess. This game reinforced the point I have been trying to make about individual differences. Not all computer games are alike, and different games call on different patterns of ability. Children are probably drawn to games that are most in keeping with their individual abilities and learning styles. As in Spy Fox, the icons are everywhere in this game, and learning to decode their use is half the problem.

What Children Get from Playing Computer Games

Computer games are exploding in variety and number. Within each category of game—action, adventure, fighting, puzzle, racing, role playing, shooter, simulation, sports, and strategy—new games and extensions of old ones are being released at an ever increasing rate.

The variety of games reinforces the point that computer games are geared to many different patterns of interests, talents, and abilities. There is a computer game for everyone.

Nonetheless it is possible to make some general points about all of these games. First, with the exception of computer games tied to curriculum content, there would seem to be little transfer of the skills acquired in playing these games to everyday practical or academic skills. Nonetheless, like crossword puzzles, these games do engage the child's active thinking and problem solving and as such provide mental exercise. These games are preferable to purely entertaining television programs and videos. Playing such games also contributes to the child's iconic literacy and his proficiency with the whole gamut of electronic media.

Last but not least, what is unique to computer games is that the player takes on a new identity. This is true whether the game is Piglet, Spy Fox, Professor Fizzwizzle, or the Warlord in the action game Battlefield. In traditional games such as checkers or Monopoly, you play as yourself. But in computer games, even the simplest ones, the player takes on a new identity (a so-called avatar), new powers, and new adversaries. It is not surprising, therefore, that on the Internet, young people now disguise their identity or take on new ones. Although this practice may foster appreciation of other people's points of view, it can also be a means of avoiding responsibility. We simply don't know, and it is hard to predict, either the short- or long-term effects of the identity facet of screen play.

Computer Games in Education

Unlike many earlier educational technologies, like teaching machines (early slower versions of contemporary computers), which were a short-lived innovation, computers are having more impact on education than any previous educational reform. They are creating, as I will discuss in the chapter on schooling, a new educational reality. While we hear a great deal about computer games that are violent and sexist, others are transforming the way in which we teach and learn. What makes computer games so attractive from an educational point of view is that they are self-motivating. From a theory of play perspective, computer games allow for student input (play), challenge and excitement (love), and learning about the world (work).

Teachers around the country are bringing certain games into their schools in a way to pique students' interest in everything from history and politics to physical fitness and music theory. Among the most popular are Firaxis Games Inc.'s Civilization, Games Take 2's Railroad Tycoon. . . and Dance Revolution from Kumani Corp. "We have to embrace the technology because that is the future," says Tim Meegan, a Chicago history teacher who uses Civilization. "You either have to get on board or get out of the way." Game developers estimate that at least 10 percent of the classrooms in the nation's 2,500 major school districts use mainstream titles for learning, up from only a handful five years ago.[9]

The integration of gaming into the classroom will expand as children who grew up playing computer games move into the classroom as teachers. In addition to its motivating power, gaming can also help solve the problem of individual differences in learning style. Until now most schools have favored children with reading and math skills. But as we saw in the examples above, some games require more reasoning, others more visual spatial abilities; action games require good visual motor coordination. If curriculum materials can be presented in different game formats that address differences in learning styles and ability patterns, we can significantly reduce school failure.

Computers and Parenting

Computer games have become part of our environment. As I have tried to show in this chapter, they are a mixed blessing. Computers and computer play have no place in the crib; that is a misuse and abuse of the technology. For preschool children and school-age children, computers, used sensibly, can serve an educational as well as an entertainment function. As parents we need to choose programs that are age appropriate and consistent with our values and beliefs. We must limit the time children—particularly those who favor hot media—watch television and play computer games. As I will argue in the next chapters, real play is essential to healthy mental, physical, and social-emotional growth and development. The challenge is to find the right balance between screen play and actual play.

In this connection, individual differences are all-important. To paraphrase Shakespeare: Some children are born active, some children become active, and some have activity thrust upon them. Some children have activity built into their genes. These are the children you cannot keep off skateboards, skis, bikes, ice skates, and surf boards. These children have a need for activity and are not easily seduced into sedentary television watching or computer game playing. The majority of children, however, fall into the category of those who learn to be active. But they can also learn to be inactive as well. Unlike innately active children, these children can be seduced into inactivity. That is why we must not allow children to spend too much time on sedentary activities. We should encourage children to be as active as possible. It troubles me, for instance, when I see parents drive their older children and teenagers to a school or a school bus that is within comfortable walking range of their home. Walking is a healthy exercise and we should encourage children to walk whenever feasible. For children who are sedentary by nature, we may have to use rewards to encourage them to maintain healthful levels of activity.

I know this is asking a lot of parents, and in the next chapter I will describe some of the pressures facing contemporary parents and how to combat them. It is these pressures that lead us into well-intentioned but unhealthy child-rearing practices.

four

Child Play and Parent Angst

A few years ago, the parent of a child at the Children's School at Tufts University (a school for preschool and early elementary children that also serves as a lab school for college students studying child development) complained about the amount of time the children spent playing. She told me that her friend's four-year-old son was in a program where he was already learning letters and numbers. This mother was concerned that her own son might not be prepared for first grade. I was mentally rehearsing my usual lecture about the educational value of play and how much children learn from it. But it was shortly after 9/11 and I couldn't get myself to go through my long litany of the academic benefits of play. Instead, I surprised myself and said, "You know they are having a good time, enjoying themselves here and now, and that is every bit as important and valuable as preparing for the future. Play is what young children do and, while we adults may be concerned only with an activity's long-term benefits, children are playing for the fun of it." I don't think I changed her mind.

Even while trying to convince her, I was aware of the hidden question behind this mother's concern: Am I doing enough for my child? As well-informed parents and grandparents, we are concerned about

63

giving our children and grandchildren intellectual stimulation as well as social experience and extracurricular opportunities. This angst, together with changes in the toys and the media available to children, has had a profound effect on children's play. Parental angst leads to the overprotection, overscheduling, and overprogramming of contemporary children. It originates in pressures unique to contemporary family life.

Parent Pressures

Parent Peer Pressure

Peer pressure usually refers to the influence of the peer group on children. Yet parents also experience powerful peer pressure. My sense is that parents often engage in hyperparenting, overprotection, and overprogramming, in part at least, because they are concerned about how their parenting looks to others. They may even do something they don't believe in because society prescribes it as the right thing to do. This kind of pressure is particularly strong when children are young. Parents are much more involved with the schooling of preschool and elementary school children than with middle schoolers. And parent peer pressure is the most powerful during these formative years. I am familiar with this parent peer pressure from my talks to parents.

Following my lectures on the importance of play, many parents raise their hands to tell me they agree. They often begin by recalling their own childhoods and the happy hours they spent outside with their friends, without adult involvement or supervision. "But," they say (and there is always a but), "things are different now. I can't really tell my son or daughter to go out and play; it really isn't safe out there." Another parent says, "I really didn't want to put my son in soccer, but all the other boys in the neighborhood are on the team and he wouldn't have anyone to play with." Other parents tout the value of the many organized activities in which they enroll their children. "In playing sports," I am told, "children learn cooperation, competition, and good sportsmanship."

There is merit in these comments. In addition, for two-parent and single-parent working families, organized after-school activities provide adult supervision when the parents aren't there. Yet parent peer pressure is at work here as well. To understand how this peer pressure works, it is helpful to recall our early adolescence.

Around the age of puberty we ascend to a new level of intellectual ability that allows us to think in abstractions, deal with multiple possibilities, and reason about contrary-to-fact conditions. It also allows us to think about other people's thinking.

Children think, but they don't think about thinking. Adolescents can think about thinking. Young teens are secretive because they appreciate that they can have private thoughts to which no one else is privy. These high-level abilities are new, and most young teens make an understandable error. They assume that other people are thinking about what they are thinking about—themselves. Young teens are preoccupied with the physical, emotional, and intellectual transformations they are undergoing. They thus create an *imaginary audience* that is every bit as evaluative of their behavior and appearance as they are themselves. This helps explain why young teens are so self-consciousness and so susceptible to peer group pressure.

The existence of the imaginary audience has been supported by my own research and that of other investigators.[1] In an early study I constructed a scale to measure this imaginary audience with items such as, "You have looked forward to going to this party for a full month, but just as you enter you notice a large grease spot on your skirt or jeans. What should you do?" We gave this scale to hundreds of children and adolescents from grade school through high school. The elementary school children answered the question by saying they would just stay at the party, as did the older adolescents. But the young adolescents said they would "stand in the dark" or "hold my hand over the spot," or "go home and get some clean clothes."[2]

When I first wrote about the imaginary audience, I thought it was limited to early adolescence. Recently, however, we have found that the imaginary audience reappears in the first year of college. College freshmen have higher imaginary audience scores than do seniors. It now appears that the audience reemerges whenever people enter a new social situation. In those circumstances we once again become egocentric.

Being a new parent is a bit like being a young adolescent or college freshman. Parents are in a new social and emotional situation. Many mothers tell me they develop a crush on their infant. Fathers experience feelings of nurturance and protectiveness they never realized they possessed. Parents' social life changes as well. They become friends with a whole new group of people, usually couples who have children of the same age. At the same time they often see less of child-free or single friends. Because of their understandable preoccupation with their new feelings and emotions and new involvement with their child, parents again fail to distinguish between what they are thinking about and what others are thinking about. They assume that other parents are observing and evaluating their child and their parenting. Consequently one of the reasons that as parents of young and school-age children are so susceptible to parent peer group pressure is that they are responding, in part at least, to an evaluative imaginary audience of peers.

There is a paradox here. Each adolescent creates his or her own imaginary audience. Every adolescent assumes he or she is an actor, and is more concerned with being observed than with observing. That is why the audience is imaginary; everyone assumes that he or she is on stage and that the others are the audience for their performance. But because everyone assumes that he or she is an actor or actress, *there is no audience*. The same is true with young parents. While they are concerned with what other parents think of them, they are just as concerned with what they think of other parents. Anxious concern about how others are evaluating their parenting, therefore, comes from within much more than it does from without.

Stories parents tell me reinforce this way of looking at parent peer pressure. After a lecture in which I described this concept of the imaginary audience, a mother told me the following anecdote. Her ten-year-old daughter was invited to a birthday sleepover at a friend's house. The plan was to have a pizza dinner, watch a rented video followed by cake, ice cream, presents, and bed. When the mother telling me this story heard what film they chose, *Thirteen*, she decided she didn't want her daughter to watch it because it was R-rated. She called the host mother and told her that she thought her daughter wasn't ready to watch that film and that she would bring her daughter over after the girls had watched the video. The host mother reconsidered and decided to rent a G-rated video instead. The mother who told me the story was obviously more concerned with her own daughter than with the audience. Her reaction encouraged the other mother to put her daughter before the audience as well and rent a more age-appropriate video.

Clearly the mother who opposed the film had a strong sense of self that enabled her to disregard the peer audience. How do you develop a strong sense of your authenticity as a parent? I learned about one way parents do this during a promotion tour for my book *The Hurried Child*. At one of the venues I met a woman who was amused when I talked about parent peer pressure. She was the mother of four children aged four to sixteen. Her husband was a missionary, and the family had just returned to the States from many years of traveling overseas. She said that she was amazed at how influenced parents were by the media and their peers. Moving around the world, her family had become very close and secure in their values and beliefs. As a result she felt no need to put her four-year-old in an academic preschool or her eight-year-old in soccer, as other parents in her neighborhood were doing. Living in strange countries without peer group support, she and her husband had learned to look to themselves in deciding what was best for their children.

I heard similar stories when I worked with American teachers and their families who were living overseas. Teachers in American schools in Europe and the Middle East meet annually to share materials, practices, and experiences. At one such conference, I had a chance to talk with teachers informally after the sessions. Their stories nicely paralleled the story I had heard from the missionary's wife. These families moved many times and were always outsiders, particularly in Middle Eastern countries. As a result, they had to rely on themselves for support, intellectual stimulation, and entertainment. These parents could be authentic because they did not have to worry about what other parents thought. In talking about their lives, they explained how they had intellectual discussions over dinner, played games in the evenings and weekends, and took family skiing vacations. These parents were able to be authentic and playful because they looked inward, rather than outward, for guidance and direction.

The point is that our concern with what other parents think about our parenting is misguided. Most people do not spend their waking hours thinking about other people; they are too busy dealing with their own issues and lives. If we appreciate that the audience we are concerned about is largely imaginary, this can free us to use our own common sense and values in making decisions about what is best for our children. If you really believe putting your four-year-old on a soccer team is a bad idea, don't do it. Perhaps if you explain your decision to other parents, they will have the strength to act on their better judgment as well.

What are the long-term effects of being authentic and acting on your own beliefs and values in parenting? Although hard data are lacking, there is anecdotal evidence. The overseas families I have kept in touch with have maintained their closeness even though they live far apart. The children have gone on to a variety of interesting, often international careers. Another kind of anecdotal evidence comes from my college students. A number of my advisees have told me that their parents would not allow a television set in the house while they were growing up. These parents insisted that their children, among other things, read and talk about the books they had read. Looking back on it, these students appreciated what their parents did, although they didn't at the time. They learned to structure their own time, engage in self-initiated play, and become motivated, enthusiastic readers. They were also among my best students. Resisting the imaginary audience of parent peer pressure is not easy. But it can pay big dividends if you decide to do so.

Parental Overinvestment

For a variety of reasons—increased contraceptive use, later age at marriage, two-parent career families, and economic considerations—families tend to be smaller than they were in the past. The data from the 2000 U.S. census showed some revealing trends. In 1970 the number of households with four or more children made up 17 percent of families. This number was down to 8 percent by 1980. By 1990 and 2000, the number had dropped to 6 percent. Of households with children, the most frequent configuration was the single-child family (16.2 million families). Families with two children came next (13.9 million families). After that the numbers dropped dramatically. Families with three children numbered only 5.2 million and those with four or more children numbered only 2.1 million.

Parents with fewer children are more emotionally invested in each child. They have more time for each child and consequently get more involved in each child's education, social life, and extracurricular activities. They take each child's successes and failures to heart and feel responsible for them. Overinvestment in our children can lead to a kind of intrusiveness in our children's lives. If this continues it can lead to resentment and rebellion in adolescence.

Overinvestment is an issue for both parents, particularly now that many fathers are taking a more active role in parenting than was true in the past. And because parents are proud of what their children are learning, they often want to showcase this in front of relatives and friends. My granddaughter Lily's parents understandably dote on her and are eager for her to show us her latest accomplishments. But this puts a lot of pressure on Lily and takes away the fun of the activity and from her sense of accomplishment. Mark Twain had Tom Sawyer say that "work is what a body is obliged to do, and play is what a body is not obliged to do." When play becomes an obligation it is no longer play. Lily's parents are still rightfully busting their buttons over her but got the message (fortunately from her and not from us) and no longer push her to perform.

Overinvestment in children leads to a kind of angst that is less common in larger families. I am the youngest of six children and was parented as much by my older sisters and brothers as by my parents. There was sibling rivalry to be sure, and I always believed my mother favored my older brother, who was good-looking and socially skilled. Yet even if that were true, she never demonstrated that in any extra attention or special privileges. And neither she nor my father ever had the time or the inclination to get deeply involved with our individual lives. We were a working-class family and my parents had enough to do keeping a roof over our heads and food on the table to worry much about our daily ups and downs. They were pleased with our achievements but did not play favorites. And because they sacrificed so much to give us a better life, we had a different attitude than many children today. We were less concerned with what our parents could do for us and more with what we could do for our parents.

Overinvestment is not necessarily a bad thing and can reflect a healthy love and commitment. It only gets us into trouble when it leads to hyperparenting, overprotection, and overprogramming.

Media Alarms

Sitting in a restaurant with our niece and her infant daughter, we noticed that the waitress was particularly attentive to the baby. When the waitress was informed that the baby was six months old, she asked whether my niece was getting much sleep. Actually her baby was quite unusual and slept most of the night without waking. The waitress shook her head in disbelief. Then she told us, "I had to take almost a year off from work. I had read about SIDS [Sudden Infant Death Syndrome] and couldn't sleep more than a couple of hours. I kept getting up and listening to see if he was still breathing. It was awful. I am so glad he is older."

Certainly SIDS is something to be concerned about, but the point of this anecdote is that parents can become overly anxious from media reports involving threats to children. Once an incident involving children is reported in the media, such incidents are assumed to be widespread and increasing. In 1981 widely publicized allegations of child abuse in a day care center in California led to a rash of reported incidents across the country. Eventually there were at least forty cases involving charges of mass molestation in day care centers. There were at least one hundred convictions, but in almost every case these were later overturned. In 1994 federal investigation of more than 12,000 charges of child molestation at day care centers did not find a single charge that could be physically substantiated.[3]

These allegations led to a spate of national programs to help children defend themselves against abuse. It even led to No Touch policies in child care facilities. None of these programs have any evidence to prove their value.

In my opinion many of these programs have done more harm than good. As a supervisor of the early childhood education program at Tufts, I visit preschools and kindergartens where my students are teaching. Usually I sit on the floor in a corner where I am out of the way but can observe what is going on. It often happens that several boys will come around and sit next to me. (Not many men work in day care centers or kindergartens.) Through their body language these boys tell me they would like a hug. Other young men make it clear, through their facial expression and physical tenseness, that they do not want to be touched. In the past, I would put my arms around boys who seemed to want or need affection and hold them close for a few moments. I don't do that any longer because I am not sure what they have been taught. It always seemed strange to me that football, basketball, and baseball players feel no embarrassment about hugging one another after a win. Yet we are not supposed to hug young children when they need that kind of comfort.

The 1999 school shootings at Columbine High School in Colorado led to the installation of metal detectors in schools around the country. The many reports of bullying and sexual encounters by children at school and on school buses have heightened parents' concern about the physical well-being of their children. While these concerns are real, they are blown way out of proportion by the media, which may fail to note the overall minuscule frequency of these incidents on a national scale. It results in a kind of distributive justice in which the many are punished for the crimes of a few.

One unintended consequence of these media alarms is that they make us reluctant to allow our children to play on their own. The frequency of abduction and attack, while no greater than in the past, may appear omnipresent when trumpeted on national television. Certainly there are dangers and risks. But I see no reason why parents can't take their children and their friends to a park or playground and let them play while they sit and observe without getting involved in their activity. Children can play safely without adult organization; they have done so as long as people have been on earth.

Role Strain

In his classic book *The Structure of Socialization*, Harvard sociologist Talcott Parsons argued that as societies become more advanced, social roles become increasingly differentiated and specialized.[4] Whereas in the past, for example, a physician dealt with a wide variety of illnesses, there are now specialists for almost every part of the body and every disease and illness. Teachers too specialize in a variety of subjects, whereas once teachers taught all subjects and many grades. Business roles have become more differentiated as businesses have grown in size. In the mom-and-pop grocery store, the owner put out the vegetables, sliced the cold cuts, and rang up sales on the register. In large supermarkets different people fulfill each of these roles.

The role of parents has become more differentiated as well. When we were an agricultural society, parents provided for the health, vocational training, and education of their children. The establishment of free public school education in the 1830s effectively removed that function from the parental role. In the beginning of the twentieth century, schools began screening for vision and hearing and checking to make sure children were vaccinated, though it was parents who brought children to get this done. Since the 1940s schools have provided services for children with special needs—a role once left to parents. The provision of free school lunches and busing removed additional parental functions. Schools now also teach sex, drug, and character education. Day care facilities, sports, art, and music coaches and teachers have absorbed still other parental functions.

Though parents could still do all of the above if they wanted to, they nevertheless have a fairly limited role, particularly as their children grow older. They are still the ones who provide health care, food, clothing, and shelter. In addition they have primary responsibility for children's emotional well-being and socialization, for teaching them manners, morals, and values. Not surprisingly, because many traditional child-rearing functions are now shared with others, parents tend to overinvest in functions that are still considered their territory. Yet because parents share child rearing with so many nonfamily members, it is not always easy to keep the roles clear. I recall a heated controversy in a day care center about whether or not the teachers should give the children their snack. The concern was that feeding children is the parents' role and the children would be confused if teachers did it. In a misguided attempt to compensate, the custodian provided the snacks.

Recognizing their limited input into many of their children's activities is a form of stress for parents. I have spoken to many parents who were unhappy with the amount of homework their children had. They felt angry because they had little control over how things are taught. They were deeply invested in their children's academic achievement but had little or no input into their schooling. A growing number of parents home-school for this reason. In the same way, many parents whose children participate in one or another sports programs are unhappy with how they are run. Too many of these programs focus on winning more than on playing and having fun. Yet parents committed to their child's enjoyment of the sport may feel that they have no right to interfere.

Role differentiation also means that roles are more complex and demanding than they were in the past. If parents are forced or freely decide to take on additional roles, the extraordinary demands can lead to *role strain*. When parents are fulfilling several different roles, they may feel anxious about not investing enough time in their parenting role. In my travels around the country talking to parents, I have discovered that many stay-at-home mothers are even busier than working mothers. And this is not just in driving their children to the doctor, sports venues, and sleepovers. Many of these mothers have taken on volunteer charity activities that consume hours of their day. Many stay-at-home moms also volunteer at their school and drive children to trips and outings. Other stay-at-home moms, and increasingly dads, are working at home in addition to taking care of the children. Stay-at-home moms and dads can suffer from role strain as much as working moms and dads do. Overinvestment in the child heightens the angst of role strain because it adds to the parents' feeling that they are not doing enough for their child.

I recall an especially poignant example of role strain. I was observing special needs children at a day care center. One of the children had come in sobbing uncontrollably, and all of the children began acting up and crying for attention. (In day care centers there is often a kind of emotional contagion; when one child is upset, all of the children are set on edge.) One little girl, however, held up stoically. I recognized her because I knew her father, who was raising three children on his own. Two were in elementary school and this daughter, the youngest, was in the center. At the end of the day, when he came to pick her up, he expected a smile and a hug. But as soon she saw him she started wailing and crying and clung to the day care worker.

I could tell he was devastated. I knew that he had a demanding job and had to go home to bathe, feed, and read to his children before putting them to bed. Afterward he looked to the other household chores. He thought his daughter's crying was occasioned by his appearance and her unwillingness to go home. He was feeling that his efforts to be a good father were for nothing. Fortunately I was able to reassure him. I told him about the day and how his daughter had kept calm and played by herself without getting upset or demanding attention. She was holding her emotions in, and only when she saw her father did she feel safe in releasing them. Indeed, after a moment, she left the day care worker, ran to him, and buried her head in his shoulder when he scooped her up. Role strain angst is compensated by moments like that.

We may not be able to reduce the number of roles we have taken on, but we can change our attitude and reduce the overinvestment angst of role strain. As you are driving home from a long day on the job, take some moments to think of something positive or fun to say when you go into the house. Transitioning from work to home is a frame shift—a major shift in setting, attitudes, and expectations. Frame shifts are always difficult, but preparing for them takes the strain off both ourselves and our children. I recall a preschool teacher who was formerly an airline stewardess. She would prepare the children for a frame switch by saying, "Okay kids, we are coming in for a landing in fifteen minutes. Finish what you are doing and put things away before we touch ground." Role strain is a feature of contemporary life. Approaching it with a sense of humor and playfulness, however, can take some of the pressure off both us and our children.

Some Effects of Parental Angst

Parental angst has a number of negative consequences if we let it get out of control and cloud our good judgment as to what is best for our children.

Hyperparenting

Whatever its origin, parental angst can result in "helicopter" parenting, with mothers and fathers hovering over their children as they go to school, take private lessons, or participate in sports. I heard of one example of hyperparenting from the headmaster of a well-known private school in Massachusetts. He had been at the school for a long time. In the beginning when he had to discipline a child, he received a lot of support from the parents. Today, however, it is a different story. It is not unusual, he said, for the family lawyer, not the parents, to show up at his office. In one school system I know of, the parents got together and had a teacher fired because she was a tough grader. This is hyperparenting with a vengeance.

Some parents get overly involved in their children's sports activities. Our children certainly want us in the bleachers when they are playing ball. But they don't want us yelling and swearing at the coach or the umpire. In the same way some parents may get overinvested in their child's schoolwork and insist on helping. Not infrequently this ends up in battles over homework. Such battles are always what Freud called "overdetermined." They become an emotional lightning rod for other angry feelings that have nothing to do with homework. As I will show in more detail in the schooling chapter, getting a teenage tutor for a elementary schoolchild can sometimes do wonders for the child's achievement and household tranquillity.

Hyperparenting can also affect the child's involvement in music or dance. Children may not have a good idea of where their talents or passions lie. They may want to take drum or guitar lessons but then, after a few lessons and often some expense, may decide to stop. We may feel that the child has made a commitment and needs to keep it. Because we are worried about the child's future we think this will set a bad precedent in the struggle to learn responsibility. We fear our child will become a dilettante at best or a bum at worst. So we insist the child continue the lessons, and another battle ensues.

The common assumption that commitment transfers from one activity to another is wrong. There is little transfer of training from one activity to another. A child who puts her things away neatly at the Montessori school does not necessarily do the same thing at home. In the same way, a child who spends the night at a friend's may behave better there than she does at home.

The child who begs for lessons should give them a decent try, at least for a few months. If it doesn't work, leave the door open and say something like, "Okay, it may not be your thing now, but if you feel you want to take it up again when you are older, we can consider it." If we recognize that children are young and need to experiment to find out where their talents lie, we can forgive a lapse or two (not many more). When I talk this way, many parents argue, "I wish my parents had forced me to play the piano because I would be able to play it now." I don't believe so. You can take a child to lessons, but you can't make him play.

Hyperparenting gets in the way of seeing our children as separate individuals and from supporting the healthy ways in which they are different from us.

Overprotection

It really hurt when you got hit with one of those cannonballs. In my childhood a cannonball was made of slices of automobile inner tube tied together to make a huge rubber band. The cannon was usually a long two-by-four with a clothespin lashed at the end to a makeshift handle. The cannonball was stretched from the clothespin to the end of the two-by-four, and was fired by opening the clothespin and releasing the missile. Believe me, when you got hit by one of those things, you knew about it. Of course we made pistols as well, which were shorter versions of the cannon, and less lethal. We did a lot of other innovative stuff, like making our own scooters and wagons with boards fastened onto rusty roller skates. And if we could coax (or snitch) a few potatoes from home, we would roast them over a fire in the woods until the skins were black and the insides mushy. We usually burned our fingers because we were in such a hurry to eat those charred treats.

This kind of play highlights changes in children's play that occurred between my childhood during the Great Depression and World War II years and the childhood of today. In general, parents of the pre–World War II era were less concerned about risks to their children's physical well-being than they were about protecting their innocence. For one thing, families were larger, homes were smaller, and there were more open spaces, fields, and woods. Children were commonly told to "go out and play." As a result, we spent a great deal of time left to our own devices. Parents allowed us to take risks and assumed that this was how we learned to deal with the real world. We got scrapes, bruises, and the occasional black eye, but that was part of growing up and learning to look after yourself.

Adult society in general and parents in particular were more concerned about our innocence. The Hayes Office censored radio programs, films, and books. *Tropic of Cancer* was not allowed to be printed or sold in the United States. One evening comedian Bob Hope's radio show went silent for a moment. He had told an off-color joke and subsequently was taken off the air. There was no *Playboy* or *Penthouse*. There was an infamous book, *Studs Lonnigan*, that we knew had some racy passages. To get to them, however, the book had to be checked out at the library, which meant we had to find a kid who could withstand the librarian's withering glare. At home, talk about a drunken uncle or crazy aunt stopped as soon as we entered the room. Nor were we ever privy to family finances, other than being told what we could not afford.

It is far different today when concern, on the surface at least, for children's physical well-being appears to outweigh worries about their innocence. Consider the rules for infant seats and safety belts in cars. Children now wear helmets when they bike and knee and wrist pads when they roller blade. These are healthy practices to be sure, but they are also indicative of a broader overprotectiveness that comes out in other ways. Parents can use cell phones to keep tabs on their children no matter where they are. Many parents sign their children up for organized team sports so that they will be sure to wear the proper equipment and play under adult supervision. In defense, it is also true that many of the bikes, roller blades, and skateboards may be more dangerous than what kids rode on in the past. And it is also true that some parents (particularly working-class parents) still allow their children to take physical risks, but it is no longer the parental norm.

Our anxiety over protecting our children's physical well-being may, in part at least, be a compensation for our relative inability to protect their psychological innocence. Indeed, the period of childhood innocence, which once lasted through the preteen years, now ends at six or seven and even earlier. Barbie, once meant for school-age girls, is now owned by my two-year-old granddaughter. For her older cousin, going on five, Barbie is already passé. Although films are rated for their appropriateness to children, the ratings are difficult to interpret. Even young children watch TV programs and movies with overt violence, sex, and foul language. Many computer games played by school-age children are sexist, violent, explicitly sexual, and rife with four-letter words. Because we have lost control over the information flow to our children, we are forced to accept their loss of innocence with the same resignation prewar parents expressed when they accepted the risks their children took in playing outdoors on their own.

This reversal of the risk–innocence commitment has had a profound effect on children's play. When children played on their own, there were many opportunities for innovation and invention, including making their own guns. (I never bought guns for my sons, but I did not interfere if they made relatively harmless ones of their own.) When we played on our own, we also learned to relate to one another and resolve our own conflicts, even if this sometimes involved fights. Protecting children's innocence did not affect our outdoor play. In contrast, our contemporary fears about children's physical well-being does affect their play. Children are not allowed to play on their own to the extent that they once were. And much of the play they do engage in is organized and run by adults. This robs children of the opportunity to innovate and learn from their risk-taking behavior. To be sure, children today still manage to play on their own, but it is now the exception and not the rule.

Overprogramming

Our parental angst over not doing enough for our children is often expressed in overprogramming. This problem is aided and abetted by the commercialization of childhood and the abundance of toys, lessons, programs, and learning materials marketed to children. In this regard parents always ask me, How much is too much? As we saw in regard to toys and screen play, many of the claims for these products have little or no research to back them up. Yet many of us, parents and grandparents alike, feel that unless we avail ourselves of these products and programs, we are not doing enough for our children or grandchildren. Given the commercial onslaught, it is difficult to decide how much is too much.

I have been working with children and families for almost fifty years, and children still develop in the same way and at the same pace. In my opinion there is no reason for any child under five or six to participate in organized sports. Being organized means that a sport has to be played at a certain time and a certain place. This makes it an obligation so that is no longer truly play. Moreover, the young child's body is less developed. Bones aren't fully calcified and muscles haven't attained full volume. Body proportions are different. The young child's head is one-fourth of his body size. Even watered-down adult sports like T-ball don't give children more exercise than they could get from self-initiated play.

Parents often counter this point with the example of Tiger Woods, arguably the Mozart of the golfing world: "Tiger's father started him playing golf when he was three, and look at him now. To be really good a child has to start early." The problem here is that you can't take the exception as the rule. Tiger Woods is a gifted athlete, and gifts can't be taught. I recall the story told about Mozart. An aspiring composer asked Mozart to teach him how to write a symphony. Mozart replied that a symphony is very complex, and the young man would be better advised to start with something simpler and gradually work toward something more elaborate. To this the young man replied, "But Mozart, you wrote a symphony when you were eight!" "That is true," Mozart replied, "But I didn't have to ask how." You can't learn giftedness.

A child in a developmentally appropriate early childhood program will get all the exercise and all the preparation for sports that she needs in the school's outdoor or indoor play area. Pumping on a swing, going up and down a slide, riding a trike, playing in the sandbox, or scrambling up a climbing structure afford age-appropriate practice for young muscles. In addition, a play area allows children to choose which activity they want to participate in and when they want to stop. They are also able to take age-appropriate risks and engage or not engage socially with other children. As I contended in Chapter 1, play is the young child's dominant mode of learning. When we take away time from that playful learning, we deprive the child of self-created learning experiences.

School-age children six years and older, in my opinion, need only three extracurricular activities to enrich their school and family experience. A child who is involved in one social activity (say, scouting), one athletic activity (soccer), and one artistic activity (guitar lessons) will still have time for spontaneous, self-initiated play. Today, however, when children have time for free play they may want to play baseball on the computer rather than on the field. We have to limit that kind of play. Children also learn a great deal from playing real games with their peers. One of the powers of play is that it gets us to exercise our bodies as well as our minds.

These guidelines include a caveat. Not all children are the same. At Tufts I am always amazed at students who carry a full academic load, get on the dean's list, serve on the student council, participate on the squash team, and befriend one of the special needs children at our day care center. Some children simply have more energy and are able to do more than others. Some schoolchildren can do well at school and have more than three extracurricular activities. Other children cannot, and when they try to do more, something usually gives. It is important to allow these children to choose the activity they are willing to give up. Sometimes they think that we are the ones who want them to do so much and are relieved to find out this is not the case.

Overprogramming is stressful and sometimes we may not be able to judge how much a child can handle. Parents often tell me that their young children want to be in beauty contests and take ballet lessons. Yet I have to wonder whether the child's purported liking for the activity is more a desire to please the parent than a genuine interest in the activity. When young children are overprogrammed, they show it in physical symptoms, including stomachaches, headaches, and hair pulling. I saw an overprogrammed six-year-old who scratched himself till he bled. The symptoms disappeared when the parents cut back on the activities and allowed him more time for free, self-initiated play.

School-age children manifest the stress of overprogramming in behavioral ways. Some children who are overprogrammed—too many outside activities for too long—begin to do poorly in school. Other children may become depressed and apathetic. For example, I have seen a number of children who were enrolled in after-school tutoring programs even though they were having no problems at school.

Some of these children become frustrated and angry at not being able to play with their friends after school. They may show their anger in fighting with their parents and refusing to go to lessons. Parents need to appreciate that children will learn as much or more from spontaneous play than they will from unnecessary tutoring.

Another form of overprogramming is sending children to instructional summer camps. Once summer camps were designed for fun and for learning social and recreational skills. But now some summer camps, responding to parental angst, have set up instructional programs. One type is dedicated to training young people in sports rather than helping them acquire self-initiated recreational skills such as swimming, boating, and hiking. The following is an advertisement for ABC (America's Baseball Camps):

> America's Baseball Camps works hard to set the standard for professional quality instruction. Our coaching philosophy is based on the most respected and freshest training concepts in baseball. You'll find ABC camps now in 95 locations throughout 14 states and three countries. Within the past five years ABC has helped over 19,000 baseball players get to the next level. . .
>
> Our instruction specifically focuses on the "Five Tool Make-up" (hitting for power, hitting for average, throwing, fielding, and speed/agility) of a baseball player, used by every Major League organization. Instruction is always positive, specific, and ranges from basic fundamentals to advanced skills.

Other summer camps turn play time into work time. Children in these camps lose the time they might otherwise have had to engage in self-initiated and spontaneous play. Some of these camps are focused on academics—prep camps that help prepare young people from everything from getting into the college of their choice to competitive debating. There are also computer camps, and camps for public speaking and acting. While young people can learn useful skills and develop friendships at these camps, there would seem to be little time for participation in the recreational sports, the bonfires and story telling that once made summer camp a truly memorable experience.

Many traditional summer camps still operate. The following advertisement illustrates what all summer camps used to be about.

Camp Carolina.   Camp Carolina, deep in the heart of the Blue Ridge Mountains, consists of 220 acres bordering Pisgah National Forest, 450,000 acres of ridges, mountains, trails and waterfalls. Our purpose is to make a boys' summer camping experience safe, fun, memorable and a valuable factor in his complete development.

Camp O-AT-KA.   Since its founding in 1906, O-AT-KA has offered a unique, rewarding summer camping experience for boys ages 7–16 years old. Today, O-AT-KA continues to provide growth and enjoyment opportunities. Quietly situated on the shores of Lake Sebago in Maine, O-AT-KA has been the place where many a lifelong friend has been made, friends return year after year, where triumph, joy, challenge and reward are daily activities.

While there are still many camps like Camp Carolina and Camp O-AT-KA, they must compete with the sports and academic camps, and some are being forced to become more skill oriented to attract campers. In my opinion what children learn in traditional summer camp—recreational and social skills—far outweighs what they gain in the skill camps. Learning is most effective when it involves play, love, and work. This kind of learning is more likely to occur in a traditional camp than in a skills camp.

Hyperparenting, overprotection, and overprogramming interfere with the healthy interaction of play, love, and work, and with the learning that accompanies their interplay. In the next chapters we look at the ways in which play, love, and work combine to foster healthy development and ways in which parents can support this coordinated activity.

II Play, Learning, and Development

five

Misunderstandings About How Young Children Learn

Some years ago I was asked to do a psychological evaluation on a child who had just been admitted to Children's Hospital in Los Angeles. The patient was a young teenage girl who had been brought up under extreme circumstances. She was discovered when her mother went to apply for welfare and brought her daughter along. An alert social worker noticed the strange-looking child and had agency officers visit the home. What they found was appalling. The girl had been kept in a twelve-foot-by-fourteen-foot room for her entire life. The room had one window with a dirty café curtain, a potty seat, a broken television set, and piles of magazines with the pictures cut out.

Jeannie (not her real name) was thirteen years old when she was discovered. Her father thought she was retarded and wanted to keep her from being institutionalized. He committed suicide soon after Jeannie was found. When I first met Jeannie she was at the 1 percentile for height and weight for her age-group. She was stooped over and walked with a halting gait. There were permanent calluses on her buttocks from being tied to a potty chair for hours on end. She had almost no speech and could only say something like "don do dah." Jeannie did not know how to chew because she had been fed only soft gruel throughout her life.

I couldn't evaluate Jeannie with any of our standard psychological tests, so I spent a few days observing her on the ward. My most vivid memory of Jeannie was from a brief outing we took to nearby Griffith Park. Jeannie appeared overwhelmed by the sights, sounds, and smells of nature. She bent down and picked a dandelion, felt it, smelled it, and twirled it in her hands. A group of picnicking students noticed this strange child and offered her an orange. She hesitated and then took it. She smelled it and rolled it in her fingers but had no idea what to do with it. I took it from her, peeled it, and offered her a section. It was only after I put a piece in my own mouth and smiled that she did likewise. An expression of delight lit up her face as a teardrop of juice ran down her chin.

On the way back to the car, we stopped at a convenience store to buy her an ice cream. Jeannie found a rack loaded with cellophane-wrapped packages of nuts and candy. She touched the packages, smelled them, and listened intently to the crinkly sound this produced. There were so many things to look at, touch, and feel that she could not stop exploring. We finally eased her out of the store and walked back to the car. Just as we approached it, a dog barked and Jeannie shuddered as if frightened. When we got back to the hospital, Jeannie rushed to the kitchen on the ward, seeking the cook with whom she had become close. It had been a lot of stimulation for her and she sought comfort by clinging to her new friend. Jeannie had spent her day learning in the way that infants and young children do—through self-initiated exploration and discovery.

I am reminded of Jeannie when I read that computer programs for infants from six months to two years are the fastest-growing software for children. And I also think of Jeannie when I read advertisements for preschools promising to tutor young children to read and do arithmetic. Exposing Jeannie to this type of instruction would have made no sense at all. She helped me understand what was wrong with these infant computer and instructional programs. They are based on three abiding misunderstandings about how infants and young children learn, and about the role adults play in their instruction.

All three misunderstandings derive from the fact that it is almost impossible for adults to put themselves in the place of preschoolers and see the world as it appears to them. Consequently we have to make assumptions about how infants and young children go about making sense of their world. Because these assumptions are wrong, they lead to ineffective (if not harmful) teaching practices. All three practices appear intuitively correct but are in fact based on misunderstandings about how infants and young children learn.

Three Misunderstandings About How Young Children Learn

The "Watch Me" Theory of Learning and Instruction

I am not well coordinated and have trouble with ball sports. Nonetheless, I once took tennis lessons to see if I could learn with proper instruction. I never became a good tennis player, but I did learn the difference between a good and a poor tennis instructor. My first tennis instructor kept telling me to watch him as he hit balls coming at us from a machine. When I tried it, the balls were more likely to hit me than I was to hit them, and I did my best to get out of harm's way. The instructor barely concealed his frustration and disdain at my cowardice and failure to learn. My next instructor was a young woman who watched as I tried unsuccessfully to hit the balls shooting at me. She then stopped the machine and showed me how to position my feet and hold the racquet. She said that it was necessary for me to concentrate on watching the ball to hit it and not getting out of its way. I worked really hard and now I can sometimes hit the ball.

The point of this anecdote is that the good teacher always watches the learner. Skilled teachers know that children can only imitate actions they can already perform. They cannot learn new, complex skills simply by imitating or watching a teacher. Imagine trying to learn to play the piano by observing a skilled piano player. With infants and young children, who are self-directed learners, the "watch me" approach often takes the form of the parent or caregiver imposing a different activity onto the one in which the child is actively engaged. In effect the parent is saying, "Never mind what you are doing, watch me." What the child learns from such instruction is that his learning priorities are not valued by those to whom he is attached. The following is an example of a mother who wanted her child to engage in play of her choosing, rather than the child's:

> A young mother sits by the cot of her first child and watches how her daughter tries over and over again to place a red cube on a blue one on its point. After a while she has watched this long enough and asks, "Where is your dolly?' The child abandons its bricks, looks for the doll and begins to lick its face–licks, licks and licks until the mother brings Teddy on the scene. "Grr, here comes dear old Teddy!" The child turns away from the doll and takes hold of Teddy. It twists him around in its hands and finally moves one leg up and down, up and down until—well until the mother becomes bored and draws the child's attention to a ball. Politely it lets itself be distracted a third time and plays with the ball. In this way the mother spends an enjoyable afternoon and is entirely unaware how she disrupts the child's perseverance and ability to concentrate. She prevents it getting used to persevering in an activity and thoroughly occupying itself with something over a long period of time.[1]

It is vitally important to support and encourage self-directed activities by the infant and young child. Even if those activities appear meaningless to us, they can have great purpose and significance for the child. These activities are not random and have a pattern and organization in keeping with the child's level of mental ability. Allowing the child time and freedom to complete these activities to her personal satisfaction nourishes that child's powers of concentration and attention. Left to her own devices, an infant or young child can spend a long time on an activity in which she is deeply immersed. We run the risk of impairing these powers if we don't respect and value the young child's self-initiated activity.

The readiness to follow the child's lead and trust his play priorities can be learned. I watched a mother interacting with her infant who was looking at something on the far side of the room. The mother tried to interest the child in several different playthings, but to no avail. After a few moments, the mother got clued in and followed her baby's gaze. The infant was focusing on a brightly colored ribbon on a table across the room. The mother went over and brought the ribbon for the infant to look at and touch. The smile of delight on her infant's face was enough to ensure that in the future this mother would take cues from her baby.

Sometimes parents get so caught up in their need to teach infants and young children that their judgment becomes clouded. In this regard, I recall watching a mother showing her eight-month-old flash cards with pictures of presidents on them. Why it is important for an eight-month-old to learn the names and faces of the presidents, and how one would expect an infant to accomplish this, is beyond my comprehension. Nonetheless, the mother kept at it despite the baby's squirming, which indicated that he had enough. Eventually he threw up, expressing my sentiments exactly. The mother, unfazed, said to me, "If you stick with it, they will come through for you." This failure to take the needs, interests, and abilities of the learner into account is at the heart of the watch me theory of instruction. This theory doesn't work with adults and it is certainly not effective with infants and young children.

Those who write computer programs for infants and toddlers fail to appreciate the power and importance of their own self-directed learning. These programs reflect the watch me approach because they don't trust the child to decide what she wants to learn. Rather, those who write the programs and the parents who buy them decide when the child should be engaged in learning, and for how long. This interferes with the child's own learning rhythms and patterns. I have serious doubts that infants and toddlers learn anything beneficial from a computer program. Any possible benefits are more than offset by what the experience does to their inclination for self-directed learning. There is really only one lesson infants and toddlers may learn from computer programs: look for guidance from the parent or even from mechanical devices rather than trust their own learning dispositions.

A telling example of the negative effects of the watch me theory of instruction is provided by a recollection of Albert Einstein. His experience was with the violin rather than computer lessons, but the principle is the same.

> I took violin lessons from age 6 to 14, but I had no luck with my teachers for whom music did not transcend mechanical practicing. I really only began to learn when I was almost 13 years old and mainly after I had fallen in love with Mozart's sonatas. The attempt to reproduce, to some extent, their artistic content, and their singular grace compelled me to improve my technique, which improvement I obtained from these sonatas without practicing systematically. I believe, on the whole, that love is a better teacher than sense of duty—with me, at least, it certainly was.[2]

Einstein's phrase that "love is a better teacher" than is sense of duty nicely captures the idea that effective learning involves self-initiated, pleasurable activities—play and love. The watch me theory is missing these ingredients.

. I have seen what the watch me approach to instruction can do to children who lack Einstein's freedom to follow his own inclinations. When I was actively engaged in clinical practice, I saw many children whom their parents described as "bored" and "unmotivated." When I interviewed these children, they often told me about experiences at school and at home when their intense involvement in a project was interrupted by a teacher or parent. After a while, these children, like the burned child who shuns the fire, avoided becoming intellectually involved. It simply hurt too much to give up a project to which they were totally committed. These children were manifesting what I came to call the Intellectually Burned Syndrome. Schools and parents were in effect saying, "Watch me. I know what, when, and for how long you should be learning." If these young people were bored and un-motivated, it was *not* because they were lazy or lacked interest in learning. They were bored and unmotivated because they had been taught that their interests and passions were of little value. And they were, not surprisingly, not about to get interested in what we adults thought they should be learning.

Watching the learner is basic to effective instruction. And it is es-sential with infants and young children, whose communication skills are limited and whose behavior is our only clue to their interests, abil-ities, and talents.

The "Little Sponge" Theory of Learning and Instruction

When my sons were small, I took them to a three-ring circus. I was looking forward to it because I remembered the thrill of my first cir-cus. I sprang for good seats, not the bleachers—all we could afford when I was a kid. When the show started, I was really ticked that my sons were not paying much attention to what was going on in the rings. Instead they kept their eyes on the vendors moving up and down the aisles selling popcorn, cotton candy, and hot dogs. I tried to draw their attention by pointing and telling them to "look at the lady in the pink dress on the elephant." Or "look at those men on the trapeze." They looked, but not for very long. My first reaction was that children today are so spoiled by television that a circus doesn't present much novelty, compared to what they have viewed on the screen.

A few weeks later, however, my sons began to talk about the circus at the dinner table. They had noticed much more than I assumed. This made me appreciate that a three-ring circus is a lot of stimulation for young children. It takes time and intellectual maturation for children to process information as quickly as adults do. At the circus there are many new things to attend to besides the acts. The tents, the clowns, the vendors, and the other families were all novel, attention-catching stimuli. While I was concentrating on the performers, my sons were responding to the array of other fresh, and therefore interesting, attractions of the circus experience.

The idea that young children learn in the same way, and as quickly as we do, is behind the "little sponge" theory of learning and instruction. This theory was given credibility when Harvard psychologist Jerome Bruner argued that "you can teach any child any subject at any age in an intellectually responsible way."[3] But that is only true if you redefine what you mean by "subject." An infant may begin to appreciate gravity, but she is far from having a knowledge of physics as we understand that concept. Gifted writers for young children are intuitively aware of this developmental difference in the level and speed of a child's information processing ability. They choose their words and pace their stories accordingly. Consider Dr. Seuss's book *Hop on Pop: The Simplest Seuss for the Youngest Use.* Each page is devoted to a few simple words in large print accompanied by an amusing sketch:

SEE

BEE

We see a bee

PAT

SAT

Pat sat on a hat

It takes a special talent to think like a child and write at a child's level of understanding and speed of processing. For most adults, who think in more complex ways, it is hard (if not impossible) to imagine the world as it is seen and heard by infants and young children.

Nonetheless, those who subscribe to the little sponge method of instruction have interpreted recent brain growth research to support their position. Brain growth is most rapid during the first few years of life. Subscribers to the little sponge method of instruction argue that the period of rapid brain growth is the time when children can learn the most and the fastest. We should, therefore, throw as much as we can at them during this "critical period." Many programs that teach children reading and math at the preschool level are based on this interpretation of brain growth research. This interpretation, however, is really not supported by the evidence.

First, as I pointed out in an earlier chapter, it is not the number of neurons that determines speed or depth of learning but their interconnections. During the early years a lot of synaptic pruning goes on so that older children actually have fewer but more interconnected neurons than the infant and young child.[4] Second, we have abundant research to the effect that young children are not intellectually ready for formal instruction in the three Rs. As we will see in the next chapter, it is only after children have attained the age of reason that they can learn verbal rules—the basis of formal instruction. A summary of European research on early childhood education submitted

to the British House of Commons is representative of the research on
this issue:

> Comparisons with other countries suggest that there is no benefit
> to starting formal instruction before the age of six. The majority of
> other European countries admit children to school at six or seven
> following a three year period of pre-school education which focuses
> on social and physical development. Yet standards of literacy and
> numeracy are generally higher in those countries than in the U.K.,
> despite our earlier starting age.[5]

Infants and young children are not little sponges who readily ab-
sorb all information thrown at them. They take more time to process
information than adults do, at a lower level of abstraction and complexity. In part this difference reflects their immature mental ability.
But it also gives evidence of the fact that their world is still new to
them—as it was for Jeannie. Infants and young children dawdle because they are looking at the world with fresh eyes and ears. They are
caught up and excited by much that we take for granted and no
longer find of interest.

The "Look Harder" Theory of Learning and Instruction

Consider the following thought experiment. As you are reading this
sentence, it appears to you that the meaning of the words is on the
page. Now read this: *Jetzt müssen Sie in die Stadt gehen.* Unless you
can read German, the meaning of those words is no longer on the
page. This little experiment makes it obvious that the meaning is not
on the page but in our heads. When we become expert at a skill, the
process becomes automatic and unconscious. In addition, we tend to
externalize the outcome or result. Even though we construct the

meaning of the words on the page, it seems to us that the meaning is objective, out there, and has nothing to do with what is going on in our heads.

In general, externalization is an adaptive process. Once we have learned a concept of, say, "dog" we tend to see "dogness" in the animal we are looking at. It would be inefficient if we had to try and figure out what a dog, a car, or a pineapple was every time we encountered one. Our tendency to externalize concepts once we have acquired them works well—except when our task is to teach infants and young children. The world seems so "out there," so independent of our mental processes, that it is difficult for us to appreciate that the infant and young child literally see the world differently than we do. When children don't see what we do, we may be tempted to believe that they are not looking hard enough. If only they looked harder, they would see it. This is not unlike our tendency to talk louder to someone who doesn't understand English. Perhaps if we say it louder, he will understand.

In my studies of perceptual development I was able to demonstrate that children indeed see the world differently than we do. In one of these studies, I used a set of drawings in which a whole was made out of distinctive parts. For example, there was a man made out of fruit with an apple for a head, a pear for a body, bananas for legs, and grapes for arms. We showed these and similar drawings to large numbers of four- to nine-year-old children. Young children recognized the parts but not the whole; they named the individual fruits but not the man. At about five or six, there is a transitional stage where children reported seeing the man but then changed their minds and named the fruits. It was only at seven or eight that children spontaneously said, "A man made out of fruit." At this age they had the mental ability to see that one and the same thing could be two things at once, an apple and a head, for instance.

Leo Tolstoy gives a sardonic description of a teacher using the look harder theory of instruction:

He (the professor) opens the book and shows the fish. "Dear children, what is this?" The poor children are delighted to see the fish, unless they already know, from other pupils, with what sauce it is to be served up. In any case they answer: "It is a fish." "No," replies the professor. (All of this is not an invention, nor a satire, but an exact account of what I have seen without exception in all of the best schools of Germany and in those English schools that have adopted this method of teaching.)

"No," says the professor. "Now what is it that you do see?" The children are silent. It must not be forgotten that they are expected to remain seated and quiet, each one in his place and that they are not to move.

"Well, what do you see?" "A book," says the most stupid child in the class. In the meantime, the most intelligent children have been asking themselves over and over again what it is that they do see; they feel that they cannot guess what the teacher wants, and that they will have to answer that this fish is not a fish, but something the name of which is unknown to them. The intelligent ones say joyfully and loudly, "Letters." "No, not at all, you must think before you speak." Again, all of the intelligent ones lapse into mournful silence; they do not even try to guess. They look at the professor's spectacles and wonder why he does not take them off instead of looking over them. "Come then, what is in the book?" All are silent. "Well, what is this thing?" "A fish," says a bold spirit. "Yes, but is it a live fish?" "No it is not alive." "Then is it dead?" "No." "Quite right; then what is this fish?" "A picture." "Quite so." All the children repeat, "It is a picture." And they think that is all. Not at all, they have to say that it is a picture which represents a fish.[6]

From an early age we ask children to name the animals they see in books. We never expect them to say, "A picture of a dog" or "a picture of a fish." The idea that it is a symbol is understood and taken for granted. We don't literally see a "picture of a fish," we see a fish. The fact that it is a picture of a fish is an abstraction, a higher-order conceptualization, of what we are doing. The professor was asking the students to see something that was in his head, not on the page.

Many infants and young children faced with computer programs and instructional videos are in much the same position as these children: they are not sure what they are supposed to be looking at or for. Often they end up being as confused and disheartened as the children in the example above. The look harder method of instruction is bad pedagogy for older children but is particularly harmful to infants and young children, who know for themselves what they have to learn. Indeed they are programmed to learn the basic adaptive skills and concepts necessary for survival. Most infants and young children have the good sense to ignore or resist such intrusions into their self-directed learning. But if adults push too intensely on the look harder materials, even infants and young children can get discouraged and give up.

Because we adults see the external world as independent of our mental activity, we fail to appreciate how much the infant and young child have to learn during the early years. We are not born knowing what things are sweet and what sour, what things are blue and what green. We are not born knowing that one and the same thing can be two things at once. As adults we have trouble believing that we do not come into the world aware that some objects fall when you let them go, and that some objects float in water while others sink. The external world seems so real that it is difficult to comprehend that young children don't see and know the same world we do. Yet they do not.

The closest analogy of the young child's experience would be visiting a foreign country for the first time, particularly one with a culture very different from our own. What hits us when we step off the plane or ship are the sights, the smells, the sounds, the textures. No travel books, movies, or TV travelogues can prepare us fully for the real thing. We have to sense it ourselves in order to make it our own. The novelty makes the experience exciting and memorable. That is why we continue to travel despite vivid portrayals of other countries in the media. For the infant and young child, the world is a new country that young children first encounter through their senses. Like Jeannie, they need time to explore and discover this new world in their own time and at their own pace.

Travelers who visit a foreign country have already acquired and automatized a basic set of concepts about time and space, about the elements, about the cosmos, about human relations. The infant and young child must master these basic conceptions as well. In addition, the child is learning to crawl, walk, and master a foreign language—his own. With so much active learning for the infant and young child to do, does it make sense to put him on a computer or in front of a television screen?

What is so troubling about many of the so-called educational toys and programs for infants and young children is their failure to appreciate the child's reality. Lapware and other programs for young children often make the look-harder mistake. Because the programmers can recognize shapes and colors in isolation on a screen they assume children can do this as well. Yet on the computer monitor or TV screen, colors and shapes are one-dimensional and appear in isolation. Infants and young children do not experience color and shape in that way. The baby associates color with an object that has shape, texture, and weight. It takes time, effort, and a lot of experimenting to distinguish between these properties. For the infant and young child, three-dimensional objects offer more valuable learning experiences than screen images do. If the infant does not respond to these images, it is not because she is not "looking hard enough"; the child may be attending to something quite different than what the adult had in mind.

The world we know is not the world of the infant and young child. During the early years of life the child does not learn by "watching," "absorbing," or "looking harder." The young child does learn by constructing and reconstructing the world through his play-generated learning experiences. In infants and young children, more than at any other age, we see the confluence of play learning and development. *Learning is the product of play-generated experiences limited only by the child's level of intellectual development.*

Learning Through Play

Young children create learning experiences through four major types of play—mastery play, innovative play, kinship play, and therapeutic play. Mastery play makes it possible for children to construct concepts and skills. Innovative play occurs when the child has mastered concepts and skills, and introduces variations. Kinship play initiates the child into the world of peer relations. Therapeutic play gives children strategies for dealing with stressful life events. I recognize that this division of play types is artificial, and I introduce it only for purposes of discussion; infants and young children don't divvy up their learning into categories. Their intellectual, social, and emotional learning occurs at the same time. So the types of play that I identify here should not be considered compartments with hard-and-fast boundaries.

Mastery Play

Perhaps the best example of how infants use play to build concepts is their construction of permanent objects—the idea that objects exist even when they are no longer present to the senses. At birth, the infant does not yet differentiate between self and world; for example, he transforms every object he touches into an object to be sucked. The baby does not treat his mother's thumb any differently than he treats his own. Only with successive experiments does the infant appreciate that what he sees passing across his vision is the same object he has been sucking. By a series of progressive coordinations the infant begins to join together the various sensations coming from the same object. In the same way, through contact with his mother's body and his own, the baby comes to distinguish himself from other beings. This process of distinguishing among and then coordinating sense impressions gives rise, toward the end of the first year, to the mental representations of objects. It is this mental representation that leads the child to the understanding of object permanence.

The infant is learning emotionally as well as intellectually. During the early months of life, most infants will let themselves be fed by anyone who holds them. But this will change toward the end of the first year of life once the child has constructed the mother (or other habitual caregiver) as a permanent object. Once this occurs, the infant attaches to the primary caregiver and only wants to be fed by Mother (or the habitual caregiver). At this stage the baby is beginning to separate her need for nourishment from her need for the person to whom she is attached. Journalist Bob Greene offers a touching description of this sudden preference for one parent over the other.

> I'm afraid she really is becoming something of a Mama's girl. She has learned that if she cries, Susan will pick her up. Susan has spent so much time with her that she is not happy unless she is in Susan's arms. And Susan has rushed to her so often Amanda knows how to get her attention.
>
> So if Susan puts her in her crib too early, if she leaves her to play on the living room floor, even if she puts her down with me and walks out of the room, Amanda will start crying.
>
> So tonight Susan was going into the kitchen to make my dinner. "Just watch her for a minute," she said and put Amanda next to me. Amanda took one look at me and decided she would rather be with Susan. And the wailing began.[7]

Just as it is easy to identify the point at which the infant masters a notion of the mother as a permanent object, it is equally so with respect to objects.

If a four- or-five-month-old infant is toying with your car keys and you cover them with a pillow, she may cry for a moment but then turn to other activities. During the succeeding months infants begin to coordinate the sight, feel, taste, and sound of an object into an integrated whole. When this happens, the infant gains the ability to create a mental representation of the object and recognize its permanence; she will lift the pillow to find the keys that are hidden under it.

Playful experimentation with hands, feet, and senses is thus the dominant mode of mastery for the infant. It is time-consuming and requires effort and cannot be hurried. As we watch the infant learner, the inappropriateness of confronting him with computers, flash cards, and educational videos becomes more than obvious. Exposing the infant to such materials puts him at risk for no purpose. The infant learns nothing from these materials, and they may inhibit his healthy experimental learning. Fortunately most infants have the good sense to ignore or attend away from such intrusions upon their self-directed mastery learning.

The importance of the child's need to actively explore the world with his body and through his senses was again brought home to me when I was asked to evaluate the child who came to be known as the "boy in the bubble." Because of a rare disease he had to live in a totally protected environment. Testing him with instruments standardized on children who live in the world made little sense. Given his limited exposure to his environment, I was curious about how he viewed it. I asked one of the nurses to have him draw a picture of his house. He was only able to draw those parts of his house that he had actually seen; he had no idea what the rest of it looked like. When I told this to one of my sons, a teenager at the time, he said, "Duh, Dad." While the result of this little task was as obvious as my son's reply suggested, we still fail to appreciate the need of the infant and young child to explore the sensorial world. The boy in the bubble, who was unable to navigate in his world, could only draw those parts of it that he had actually perceived.

Infants and young children also create games as an aid to conceptual mastery. At four or five months the infant often creates a game by dropping a rattle on the floor; the parent responds by retrieving it. The infant is learning about the color and shape of the rattle as well as its feel and how easy or hard it is to grasp. In addition, the infant is learning that things fall down when you drop them and make different noises when you drop them from different places. Equally important is the social learning that is going on. The infant learns that the adult will retrieve the rattle if she drops it. The infant also learns that if she continues the game long enough, it will test the parent's patience.

Infants often play banging games as a way of learning to conceptualize objects. Give the six-month-old a rattle and he will bang it on the eating tray. If you replace the rattle with a wooden spoon, it too will become an object to be banged. Offer the child a teddy bear. . . and it will be banged against the tray.

Now the child learns that some things don't make loud sounds when you bang them. With this game the infant is practicing motor skills also. But that changes over the next few months when the infant becomes interested in the objects themselves rather than their banging possibilities. By the end of the first year, the infant makes a game of exploring the various features of the object by passing it from hand to hand while examining it.

Although infants create many games, parents can initiate games that build on the infant's growing ability to understand object permanence. Such games simply reinforce learning processes already under way. Games such as peekaboo in which we look at the baby and then duck out of sight help the child construct mental representations of absent objects. In the same way games like "Pat a cake, pat a cake, baker's man, bake me a cake as fast as you can" fits with the child's need for rhyme and repetition. If you clap your hands to the song, the infant will clap along. Such games support the baby's improved motor abilities, provide language stimulation, support the baby's sense of rhythm, and create enjoyment.

Once infants have constructed permanent objects, they use play to order these objects into groups. The following observation by a god-mother is an example:

> From the age of twelve months, my godson devoted himself for many weeks to his own game with space and quantity. Whenever he had a large number of similar things at his disposal, such as balls, little bricks, plums or other fruit, or even six shining red plastic plates, he would distribute these objects around the room. He would look at the result for a while and then head for each piece on his unsteady legs, laboriously pick it up, and gather all of them together again. Then he would look with satisfaction at what he had collected and, after a moment, start to distribute them all over again. Still more pleasing than the rattle of the plates or the rolling of the plums was the way in which paper handkerchiefs floated silently to the ground. There they lay, silent and flat on the carpet until they were again heaped as a loose mass on the sofa. For weeks, the mother wisely left the child at these games.[8]

Once children come to understand that objects are permanent, they start to group those which are alike and those which are differ-ent, the beginnings of classification. Children will engage in this all-important intellectual activity on their own for long periods of time if given the materials and freedom to do so. The infant's mastery is or-ganized and purposeful, even if it is not obvious to us.

Repetitive Play and the Mastery of Motor Skills

Infants and young children exemplify the adage "practice makes perfect." Repetitive play is one of the ways in which children master major motor skills.

We see this at different age levels. About the time my granddaughter Lily began to walk, she also wanted to climb the stairs at our house—there were none in her parents' ranch house. She laboriously made her way up the stairs, and I helped her down. She wanted to go up them again and again. The next time the family visited, several months later, she indicated that she wanted to go down by herself as well. While I held her hand and she held the railing we walked down the stairs, and repeated this exercise many times. I had a similar experience with my granddaughter Heather when she was about the same age.

Stairs are a natural challenge to young children, and they will try to climb up and down them if they are available. Children seem to know that going up and down stairs gives them practice in a number of skills that they do not acquire from walking on a single plane. Going up and down the stairs requires children to coordinate climbing with the visual clues of the height of each stair. It is one of the challenges that makes stair climbing so attractive. A. A. Milne, one of those writers gifted in seeing the world as a child, gives us a sense of what stair climbing is to a child:

> Halfway down the stairs is a stair where I sit.
> There isn't any other stair quite like it.
> I'm not at the bottom, I'm not at the top.
> So this is the stair where I always stop.

Self-initiated repetitive practice as a learning mode appears at later ages as well. Montessori gives a telling example of a child absorbed in repetitive mastery play. One day when Montessori was visiting Casa dei Bambini (the children's school she founded in Rome), she noticed a little girl of about three intently fitting the graded cylinders into their proper places in the containers, taking them out, mixing them up, and then starting all over again. She repeated this exercise over and over, totally involved in what she was doing and oblivious to what was going on around her. Montessori writes:

> I then decided to see how concentrated she was in her strange em-
> ployment. I told the teacher to have the other children sing and
> march around her. But this did not disturb the child at all in her
> labors. I then gently picked up the little chair in which she was sit-
> ting and set it on a small table. As I lifted the chair she clutched the
> objects with which she was working and placed them on her knees,
> but then continued with the same task. From time to time I began
> to count; she repeated the exercise forty-two times. Then she
> stopped as if coming out of a dream and smiled happily. Her eyes
> shone brightly and she looked about her. She had not even noticed
> what we had done to disturb her. For no apparent reason, her task
> was finished. But what was finished and why?[9]

Montessori's question is an important one. It reiterates the point that the child knows the meaning and purpose of her actions, even if they seem mysterious to us. Early childhood educator Joan Almon offers another example of self-initiated repetitive play associated with a skill. This one had a goal and outcome that the observer could appreciate.

> Four-year-old Ivana came to kindergarten one Monday morning
> and proudly announced that she could tie her shoes. I must have
> looked skeptical because it is beyond the skill level of most chil-
> dren her age. Ivana—determined to demonstrate her new

prowess—promptly sat down on the floor and untied and then retied her shoes into perfect bows, looked at my astonished face and beamed. Later in the day I asked her mother how Ivana had learned to do this. Her mother laughed and described how over the weekend Ivana had pretended that she was going to a birthday party. She folded scraps of paper into little birthday packages. She then raided her mother's yarn basket and used pieces of yarn to tie the packages with bows. She probably tied sixty or seventy packages until she had at last mastered the art of tying bows. She clearly felt ready and did her work in the spirit of play. If someone had required Ivana to tie her shoes before she signaled her readiness and interest, and proceeded to give her formal instruction, learning would have been transformed into a tedious and stressful task.[10]

Skill Mastery and Innovative Play

Once children have mastered a skill by repetitive play, they want to innovate and push the limits of their newfound skill. Watch a child learning to climb up to the top of a slide and go down. Initially the child will repeat the process over and over again. Then, extending the limits of what he has learned, the child may try climbing up the slide rather than the stairs; some children try going down on their stomachs. Once children feel confident walking, they want to run and to jump. In the same way, an older child who has learned to ride a bike will then experiment riding without hands, going on one wheel, and so on. Adults too, when they have mastered a skill, want to push the limits. That's when skiers are likely to break a leg.

It is not only the mastery of motor skills that gives rise to innovative play. We can observe it with language skills as well. A personal example can illustrate this function of innovative play. When one of my sons was a preschooler, he had great difficulty pronouncing the sound of the letter *l*. He would say "yayoo" for yellow. His older brother would tease him and say "yayoo" back to him. Bobby would then reply in exasperation, "Not yayoo, yayoo." He could hear the sound but could not pronounce it. One day I came home from the office to find Bobby at the kitchen table, working on a drawing—his favorite pastime. While he was drawing, he was singing a song he had just made up: "Yellow, yellow, yellow, it's so easy to say yellow." He had mastered the *l* sound and made up a song to celebrate his victory.

A similar kind of innovative play occurs later when children reach a new level of understanding of name-calling. When children reach this stage they are likely to sing, "Sticks and stones will break my bones but names will never hurt me." Once children become more advanced verbally we see many different forms of word play, of going beyond the usual word meanings. They start to understand and pose riddles.

What is the difference between a piano and a fish?
   You can't tuna fish.

What did the octopus say to his date?
   I want to hold your hand, hand, hand, hand, hand.

What do cows give after earthquakes?
   Milkshakes.

Play thus serves not only as a means of learning skills but also as a way of expanding and elaborating them. This is not surprising. It is only after the artist or the scientist has mastered the basic skills of the discipline that she is ready to innovate and go beyond and challenge the frontiers of what has been already learned. Even a painter like Jackson Pollock, whose work seems at first glance to be nothing more than splashed paint, was trained in the classical mode before he innovated in his unique way.

Kinship Play

When our granddaughter Lily was three, we took her to the Frog Pond in the Boston garden. It is a shallow wading pond with a huge fountain spraying water for the children to jump under. No sooner was Lily in the water then she found a friend, a little boy of about the same age. They held hands, splashed in the water, and then splashed each other. They took turns chasing each other in the water and then used their baseball caps to scoop up water and pour it out. Neither child spoke much, although Lily is quite verbal and the other child was too, from what I could hear him say to his mother. What is so striking about such play is that it is between two children who are complete strangers, yet behaving as if they were longtime friends. This is kinship play.

Children of about the same age and size are naturally drawn to one another. They share a common pint-size view of the world, a common subordination to adult authority, and a common wish to relate to someone like themselves. It is a kinship bond that I have observed with my children and grandchildren. Children who don't know one another communicate through self-initiated games. These games are fun because the children are at the same skill level and because it is a relationship of mutual rather than unilateral authority (as with adults). Kinship play is an initiation into social learning and cooperative activities. Interestingly, children who show stranger anxiety with adults do not show this fear with strange children of the same age. Part of this kinship bond is the sense that someone of the same size can be trusted.

Kinship play is easy to understand. If we are in a foreign country with few other tourists, meeting a fellow American is delightful. Even as strangers, we share a common language, culture, food preferences, sport enthusiasms, and so on. Under such circumstances friendship bonds can develop quickly. It is a sense of fellow countryman kinship that draws us to people from the States when we are abroad. Young children live in a world that is engineered for the minds and bodies of adults. As foreigners in this country, young children find comfort and reassurance in meeting and engaging with someone of their own kind. In kinship play, they discover a sense of mutuality that they will elaborate in all future peer relationships. Unlike adults, they can do this abroad without sharing a common language or culture.

Therapeutic Play

When we think of play therapy, we often associate its use in the clinic with troubled children. But all children use play therapeutically as a way of dealing with stress. For example, one of the baby's earliest traumas occurs after the mother can be represented in her absence. Although the infant can mentally represent the mother, the baby knows it is not the same as when she is present. When the mother disappears, the infant fears that she may not return. Psychiatrist Selma Freiburg insightfully described the therapeutic function of peekaboo play for children dealing with their first experience of separation anxiety:

> What is his favorite game during this period of development? Peek a Boo and all the variations of this game will occupy the baby interminably. He will play the game by pulling a diaper or his bib over his face, and then pull it off with cries of delight. He will play hiding games with any cooperative adult, watching them disappear with a solemn expression on his face, greeting their return with joyful screams. He can keep up such games longer than you can.
>
> What is the pleasure of these games? If the disappearance and return of loved ones is such a problem to him, why should the baby turn all of this into a boisterous game? The game serves several purposes. First by repeating the disappearance and return under

conditions that he can control (the missing person can always be discovered again after brief waiting), he is helping himself overcome the anxiety associated with this problem. Secondly, the game allows him to turn a situation that would, in reality, be painful into a pleasurable experience.[11]

A similar trauma occurs when the mother becomes pregnant with another child. Psychologist Bruno Bettelheim gives an illustration of how one girl used play to help her cope with this disturbing development.

A four-year-old girl reacted to her mother's pregnancy by regressing. Although she had been well trained, she began to wet again; she insisted on being fed only from a baby bottle and reverted to crawling on the floor. All of this greatly distressed the mother, who, looking forward to the demands of a new infant, had counted on her daughter's maturity to make this easier. Fortunately, she did not try to prevent these regressions, something which would have been difficult, as the child was not just playing at being an infant again, but insisted upon acting as one.

After a few months of this regressive behavior, the girl replaced it with much more mature play. She now played the "Good Mother." She became extremely caring for her baby doll, ministering to it in a variety of ways and much more seriously than ever before. Having, in the regressed stage, identified with the coming infant, in now what was clearly play, she identified with her mother. By the time her sibling was born, the girl had done much of the work needed for her to cope with the change in the family and her position in it. Her adjustment to the new baby was easier than the mother had expected and feared.[12]

Sometimes a child's play can help the child deal with impulses that are socially unacceptable. Imaginary companions may serve as fantasy surrogates of the child's wild side. Dr. Freiburg gives a telling example of this type of therapeutic play as well.

He acquires a number of companions, imaginary ones, who personify his vices like characters in a morality play. (The virtues he keeps to himself, Charity, Good Works, Truth, Altruism, all dwell in harmony within him.) Hate, Selfishness, Uncleanliness, Envy and a host of other evils are cast out like devils and forced to obtain other hosts.

"I don't like Gerald, Gerald bites," Stevie reports at the dinner table. "Who's Gerald?" says his mother, puzzled. "Gerald is my friend." "Where does he live?" says Mama, not catching on. "In the basement," says Stevie. "Does Stevie bite when he gets mad?" his father asks shrewdly. "Oh, not Stevie," says the boy named Stevie. "Stevie is a good boy." And adds loyally, "Stevie is my friend."

In this way Gerald comes to live in the house and can be counted on to complicate family living. When Daddy's pipes are broken, no one is more indignant than the two-year-old son who is under suspicion. "Gerald, did you break my Daddy's pipes? He demands to know." Gerald can offer nothing in defense and it is plain as the nose on Gerald's face that only he could have committed this heinous crime.[13]

This use of imaginary companions is not unique and is probably universal as attested to by the following example of a Russian child, reported by the beloved Russian children's author Korney Chukovsky:

I first came across this amazing example of it (the joy of using language correctly and deep embarrassment over errors) when Yurik, two and a half years old, once made a slip of the tongue and said instead of "screw"—"shew." When corrected, he said unabashedly: "Boris said 'shew' but Yurik said 'screw.'"

This Yurik did not number among his acquaintances a single Boris. He invented a Boris for the express purpose of pinning on him all of his mistakes and blunders, crediting himself only with faultless speech. "It's Boris who said 'mamovar'; Yurik always says 'samovar.'" Inventing Boris, the shrewd tot ensured for himself complete peace of soul. Thanks to this legendary Boris, he himself remained, under all circumstances, an infallible authority on spoken Russian, enjoying, in addition, the satisfaction of ridiculing a defeated "competitor." By means of this machination, a two-and-a-half-year-old child shielded his sensitive ego—he had found his mistakes so embarrassing that he had to invent a double to burden with his mistakes.

The more I looked into this matter the more I was convinced that Yurik was not an exception to the rule. The French novelist Georges Duhamel tells a similar story about a three-year-old Parisienne. He wrote, "She was terribly mischievous, cunning and resourceful. She experimented with adult speech and, to avoid responsibility, she blamed all of her errors on an imaginary brother." This is exactly what Yurik did.[14]

In this example, the child's imaginary companion takes the blame for his inventor's linguistic errors. It reflects the child's intense need to use language accurately, which was also evidenced by the example of my son Bobby and his inability to say "yellow."

Mastery play is the dominant learning orientation of infants and young children. All of their experiences are fresh, novel, and exciting. During the first years of their lives young children are quite literally visiting a foreign country. And, because young children do not think in adult concepts and categories, they approach this new land from many different perspectives at the same time. They see this new world as artist, naturalist, writer, scientist, and much more. That is why young children are so fascinating to watch. One moment the child is a naturalist busily examining a grasshopper, the next an artist putting impressions on paper, the next a writer describing an experience in highly original language, and always the sociologist exploring the potential of social interaction. These many roles are fulfilled with joyous excitement. This is why it makes no sense to rush infants and young children into computers, television, and academics. Why intrude on a time when children are so primed to learn what they need to learn with joy and enthusiasm?

As children transition from early childhood into the elementary school years, their play takes on new functions as it becomes subordinate to the dominant disposition of this age period—work. In this context work is acquiring the basics of literacy, math, and science.

six

Playing for a Reason: Building the Units of Math, Reading, and Science

W hen our sons were small, they were always fighting. One Saturday it was raining hard and our oldest son, Paul, could not join his friends for a planned outing. His mother prevailed on him to play a game of Chutes and Ladders with his four-year-old brother, Bobby. After some persuading and cajoling to the effect that it was not beneath a seven-year-old to play with a four-year-old, he agreed. The game was set up on the floor of the family room and the boys' delighted mother set out milk and cookies as rations for the mighty contenders. Her vision of peace and tranquillity, however, was short-lived. From the family room, Paul shouted out, "I'm not going to play with him; he cheats."

Paul was playing according to the rules of the game: you move your token as many places as the spinner says. If the spinner says three, you move your token three spaces. To learn and follow such a rule, a child has to attain what the ancients called the "age of reason," usually around six or seven and coincident with the loss of baby teeth. This form of reasoning is exemplified by the classic syllogism.

All men are mortal (major premise) (You move your token as many spaces as the spinner says)
Socrates is a man (minor premise) (The spinner says three)
Socrates is mortal (conclusion) (You move your token three spaces)

But Bobby was not there yet. At his age he knew only one rule: "I win, you lose." It wasn't really cheating when he moved his token more spaces than the spinner said because he was not intentionally breaking the rule. His brother, however, did what we all tend to do when people fail to follow the rules: we attribute bad motives to their behavior.

It is simply a fact that young children think differently than older children and adults. Their mode of thinking is concrete and is sometimes called *mythic* or *syncretic*. For example, one of my sons once asked me, "Daddy, if I eat spaghetti will I become Italian?" A Russian child visiting the far north, where the summer sun shines most of the night, implored, "Mama, please turn off the sun; I want to go to sleep." In these forms of thought there are no levels of conceptualization and everything is on the same plane (e.g., eating spaghetti and becoming Italian). And it includes the belief that adults are all-powerful and all-knowing. ("Mommy, turn off the sun.") We also see this concreteness in the young child's definitions, "a hole is to dig" and "a bike is to ride." Likewise a young child will describe things in nonquantitative ways: the mama block and the baby block. This form of thinking is not wrong; it is simply different from our own. It is age appropriate and children will move out of it at their own time and pace.

The movement from mythic/syncretic thought to rational thought is aided and abetted by the forms of play described in the previous chapter. One of the confusing aspects of this development is that language skills often race ahead of the child's reasoning abilities. The same child who can speak in complex sentences cannot yet follow verbal rules. My granddaughter Lily is bilingual and at age four speaks in complete sentences—she knows the rules of language, noun before verb, and so on. Yet when she played with her six-year-old cousin, she was not able to follow the rules of a board game. It is only when young children have to follow explicit *verbal* rules that require reasoning that we see this discrepancy between language growth and intellectual development. Parents and grandparents are often misled by a young child's verbal precocity and assume that it is an index of intellectual giftedness. Most often it is not. An easy check is to ask the child to draw or copy a diamond. You will be surprised. I'll explain the difficulty in drawing a diamond later.

As well as marking the transition into the age of reason, the years from four to six mark a shift in the three dispositions of play, love, and work. Learning the tool skills of reading, writing, arithmetic, and computers brings work to the forefront. But play and love are still important. Children make the most progress when all three dispositions are involved in their learning and instruction.

The Age of Reason

The Tools of Reason

In ancient times, reason was defined in terms of Aristotle's syllogistic reasoning, illustrated by the breakdown given above. When the ancients spoke of the age of reason they were using the term "age" in a generic way, much as we speak of the "computer age." They recognized that this age covers a broad time period and that children attain the ability to reason, like their permanent teeth, at different chronological ages. Swiss psychologist Jean Piaget described this reasoning as the stage of "concrete operations."[1] Using experiments that have since been duplicated throughout the world, Piaget demonstrated what the ancients had determined solely from observation: the age range at which children attain these new mental abilities is roughly between five and seven, and varies from child to child.[2]

An analogy may help make this point. Intellectual growth in early childhood is much like the period of rapid physiological and physical growth in early adolescence. Some young people attain puberty at eleven, some at twelve, some at thirteen, some at fourteen, and some even later. We all attain puberty, but at different rates depending largely on genetic background. Early maturers tend to have parents who matured early, and the same is true for later maturers. In young children the same holds true. Some children attain the age of reason at four, more at five, and most by six. That is why it makes little sense to instruct young children according to their chronological age rather than their developmental level.

The ancients made the attainment of reason the prerequisite for formal instruction. They recognized that all formal instruction involves the inculcation of *rules*. The same is true today. In reading, for example, there are any number of phonetic rules: when two vowels go walking the first one does the talking or *i* before *e* except after *c*. And so on. In math children learn the place rule. The same number can stand for single units, units of ten, or units of one hundred depending on its spatial position. In science too, rules are fundamental. Equations are basically rules. The equation

speed = distance/time

is essentially a rule for determining the time it takes to cover a specific distance.

Syllogistic reasoning also enables the child to understand that *one thing can be two things at the same time*. The young child's difficulty with relations illustrates this point. For example, when my youngest son Rick was a preschooler I asked him, "Do you have any brothers?" he replied yes and named them. Then I asked him, "Do your brothers have any brothers?" "No," he said. At the level of syncretic thinking you cannot *have* a brother and *be* a brother at the same time. Suppose you ask a preschooler how many boys and girls are in her nursery class. The child may be able to count them and say correctly that there are "ten girls and seven boys." (Children often know these numbers because they help take the roll.) If you then ask the child, "Are there more girls than boys?" she can usually answer correctly that there are more girls. But the child is puzzled if you ask, "Are there more girls than children?" and in response repeats, "There are more girls than boys." Without syllogistic reasoning the child cannot appreciate that you can be a child and a boy or a girl at the same time.

The idea that one thing can be two things at the same time is a byproduct of the rules described earlier. The rule that "when two vowels go walking the first one does the talking" means whether or not a letter is sounded depends on the order in which it appears. In math, the same number can represent single units or ten units or a hundred units, depending on its spatial position. In physics the speed equation means that speed can be attained by combinations of different time and distance units. Although there are fewer rules in geography, the child must grasp that one same map line can define the boundary of two different states or countries. Reasoning tools are a prerequisite for formal instruction.

The Age of Reason and Child Rearing

As parents we want to know when our children have attained the age of reason. For example, we want our children to learn the rule that "whenever you ask for something, you say 'please' and whenever someone gives you something, you say 'thank-you.'" Sometimes children learn to do this because of the context—mealtime—but sometimes they "forget." They don't really forget; they just have not attained the abilities needed to learn the general rule. Of course we should continue to encourage children to use manners before they learn the verbal rules. But we should not attribute bad motives to their behavior if they "forget" when they don't have sufficient contextual clues to guide them.

Young children have the same problem with many other rules we try to inculcate, such as putting their toys away, picking up things they have dropped, not getting up from the table, and so on. If we appreciate that these lapses reflect intellectual immaturity rather than stubbornness or rebellion, we can handle them in a playful way. When we do this, the child is more likely to learn the rule than if we criticize the child for something he cannot help. Introducing an imaginary mediator is one way of doing this. You might say, for example, "Mr. Rabbit tells me that when you get a little older you will be able to remember to pick up your toys when you are finished playing." Or, "Mr. Rabbit tells me that when you get older, you will not leave the table without asking." In this way we recognize the child's immaturity in an accepting and humorous way, while helping the child anticipate being able to comply in the future. Using a mediator also makes us appear less the ogre. Here we take a page from the child's book and make an imaginary authority the "bad guy."

The young child gives us many clues to her level of development. If, for example, a young child is surprised to see her nursery school teacher in the supermarket it is likely because she is thinking, "How can you be a teacher and a regular person at the same time?" If our preschooler is taken aback to see us dressed up, (or in sweat pants depending upon what we usually wear in their presence) it is for the same reason. Another clue to a child's level of development is his or her story preferences. The child before the age of reason prefers fairy tale characters because they are one-dimensional. The fairy godmother is good, kind, and gentle. The wicked ogre is ugly, mean, and selfish. Goldilocks is a bad girl. In the unexpurgated edition, she jumps out the window and breaks her neck when the bears catch her in their beds. Before the child attains syllogistic reasoning, he prefers rhymes and poems that are simple sequences of events:

Little Jack Horner sat in a corner
Eating a Christmas pie,
He put in his thumb and took out a plum
And said, "What a good boy am I!"

Little Boy Blue, come blow your horn,
The sheep's in the meadow, the cow's in the corn.
Where's the boy that looks after the sheep?
He's under a haystack fast asleep.
Will you wake him? No, not I;
For if I do, he's sure to cry.

In these rhymes, like all rhymes, poems, and stories for young children, the times and places are very general, very concrete, and very here and now. They are playful in the sense that they have amusing, unexpected outcomes. When young children lose interest in this kind of story or poetry, it is a good sign that they have moved to the next level of intellectual development.

To illustrate, when children enjoy hearing or reading about Winnie the Pooh, this is a good sign that they have attained syllogistic reasoning. Pooh is a nice fellow but sometimes forgets things; for example, he absentmindedly eats Eeyore's birthday present. So he is a good little bear, but he has his faults. At this age children want more complicated characters and more involved plotlines. Children's language also gives clues that they have moved to a higher level of thinking. If you ask a preschooler to describe three blocks of different sizes, he is likely to say, "This (the biggest block) is the daddy, this (the next biggest block) is the mommy, and this (the smallest block) is the baby." A child who has attained the age of reason might describe the same blocks differently: "This one is the tallest and fattest, this is one is the next tallest and fattest, and the little one is the shortest and thinnest." Now that the older child can reason syllogistically, he can use two dimensions in describing the blocks.

The Age of Reason and Formal Instruction

Knowing whether or not the child has made the leap to syllogistic reasoning is crucial to the introduction of formal instruction in reading and math. The preschooler is eager to learn the names of the letters and some sight words. The young child is just as avid about learning numbers and counting. Such learning is well within the presyllogistic child's level of competence. It is simply an extension of the young child's natural disposition for learning the names of plants, animals, colors, shapes, and forms. Formal instruction in the tool skills is another matter. The child has no built-in predisposition to learn that "when two vowels go walking the first one does the talking." Once we introduce formal instruction, we can no longer rely on the child's own dispositions and motivations.

To ensure motivation and avoid frustration, we need to be confident that children have their reasoning skills before we introduce formal instruction. This is true not just for academics but also for music and sports. In the Suzuki method of teaching violin, for example, the children are not taught to read notes. The method recognizes that reading notes is too difficult for preschool children. In the same way, T-ball was invented for younger players. Hitting a moving ball requires a level of visual–motor coordination that is beyond most preschoolers' competence. The ability to grasp that one thing can be two things is a necessary but not a sufficient condition for children to learn the rules of sports and music as well as those of literacy and numeracy.

Children are not naturally motivated to learn from formal instruction. This motivation comes first and foremost from the ways in which literacy, math, music, and sports are introduced. Formal instruction is work. For it to be effective, play and love need to be made part of the process. Parents and teachers are most effective if they build on children's love of stories, contrasts, rhythm and rhyme, unexpected facts, and humor. If we introduce literacy and numeracy with the use of these techniques, we build on children's spontaneous motivation and make learning interesting and fun. At the same time, we also win the child's respect and affection and thus make the instruction a matter of play and love as well as work.

Given that the child has attained the age of reason and is fortunate enough to have parents and teachers who introduce reading and math in interesting ways, there is another factor to consider. Children who have attained the age of reason may still be at different levels of proficiency with this kind of thought. For example, children who have spent a great deal of time watching television may not have the auditory discrimination skills necessary for decoding phonics. With television children follow the law of least effort—get the information as easily as possible. Because it is easier to get information visually, children often pay little attention to the language used by the TV characters. So, even though a child has attained the age of reason, he or she may not be able to use it effectively in learning certain basic skills. With young children, the teaching has to be flexible and open to the fact that even children who have attained the age of reason may still vary in their ability to put these tools to use.

I can't close this section without a poem by A. A. Milne which is his way of describing the attainment of the age of reason.

When I was one, I had just begun.
When I was two, I was nearly new.
When I was three, I was hardly me.

When I was four, I was not much more.
When I was five, I was just alive.
But now I am six, I'm as clever as clever.
So I think I'll be six forever and ever.

Attaining the Age of Reason

Self-directed play experiences nourish and support the child's maturing mental abilities. As I suggested in the discussion of mastery play, such play aids the construction of concepts like object permanence as well as reasoning tools like classification and ordination (ordering things according to size). These are the activities that facilitate the growth of a child's reasoning abilities. Mastery play is first and foremost concerned with adaptation, with helping the child navigate in the new world she has been thrust into. We can see this adaptive process as the child encounters the elements, plants, and animals, observes the moon and stars, and playacts. These are a few of the aspects of the natural world the young child is exploring and trying to understand. By comparison with this natural world, what young children are offered by a video or computer program appears both shallow and barren.

To help us appreciate how the world looks to the young child and how he adapts to it, I will use, among other things, children's questions that highlight their abiding curiosity and wonder about the world. Children's questions are a form of mastery play; in asking questions, children are creating their own learning experiences.

The Elements

Earth, water, air, and fire present new and challenging experiences to young children and help them understand that one and the same thing can be different things at once. Many children first encounter the earth in in a sandbox. They can make the sand into many different forms and shapes using cups, boxes, and the like. Sand can also be poured over a toy waterwheel to make it turn and it can also be pasted on paper to make a rough surface. Some children are fortunate to encounter sand at the beach where they cover themselves with it or build trenches for the water to run into when the tide rises. Some first play with earth in the form of mud and find that they can use it to paint their faces or make mud pies. In the garden, children learn that earth is where the plants grow.

Water. Water is endlessly fascinating to young children because it serves many different functions. You can drink it when you are thirsty, wash yourself with it when you are dirty, and wade in it when you are hot. Water can also be colored and sweetened when you make it into lemonade. Children also discover that water can be frozen into ice to cool things and boiled to cook things. It can float toys in a bath tub and you can even squirt it with a gun. Water also takes the form of rain, snow, and icicles. As children engage in water play, they are learning the many different ways that water can be the same but different.

Children's questions also reflect their curiosity about rain, "What makes rain? How does the water get up in the sky? What's evaporation? Why does it come down? Where does it go? What does the ground do with it?"

Air. Young children notice the presence of air when they feel it brush against their skin when someone moves close to them. Later they will watch while some things float gently to the ground while others fall quickly. Young children also begin to note changes in temperature during the day and at night. While they are not fully aware of what this medium is, they are aware that they are immersed in something that changes from warm to cold and is related to the rate at which things fall. Even infants are fascinated as they experiment with dropping paper, which floats slowly, and a ball, which drops quickly. Balloons also fascinate young children as they watch adults blow them up. Children will find another function of the air when they learn to fly kites and paper airplanes. Through all of these play activities children come to know not only about air but that it—like earth and water—can be used in different ways.

Gifted authors for children have a special talent for seeing the world as children do and the adaptive problems it poses for them. They often highlight facets of experience young children are dealing with that we may not think of. Some of the ways that children observe the presence of air are suggested in a book titled *All Falling Down.*

Petals fall from flowers, gently on the table, gaily in the wind.
Water falls from the fountain into the pool where little birds bathe
and fishes swim.
Apples fall down and children put them in baskets.
Leaves fall down and men rake up the leaves in piles.
Nuts fall down; squirrels gather the nuts they find.[3]

Here is a poem that reflects children's questions about the wind.

WHO HAS SEEN THE WIND?
Who has seen the wind?
Neither I nor you:
But when the leaves hang trembling,
The wind is passing through.
Who has seen the wind?
Neither you nor I:
But when the trees bow down their heads,
The wind is passing by.[4]

Young children are curious about extremes of weather like hurricanes, tornadoes, and earthquakes. In answering children's questions about this subject, we need to remember their mythic thinking. Young children assume that everything has a purpose. Thus to a question about hurricanes we might respond, "Hurricanes remind us to be careful when we build houses so that they won't get blown down." (The story of the three little pigs is a good example here.) We can use the same type of explanation for tornadoes and earthquakes. Detailed scientific explanations will only confuse children. These purposeful explanations are not wrong; they are just the most relevant to someone who has yet to attain the age of reason.

Fire.   Children are exposed to fire at a later age. This seems only natural, since manmade fire came later in human history than the earth, water, or air. When children are exposed to fire, whether on a gas stove, a candle, or a fireplace, they are fascinated by it. Fire is mysterious; it presents moving colors and gives off heat. As with the other elements, young children gradually learn the many functions of fire—to give off light, cook things, and burn things up. They also learn that fire can hurt if they accidentally burn themselves. Children need to learn about the dangers of fire but also about the many useful purposes it serves in everyday life.

Children cannot help but create learning experiences with the elements. Through playing with sand and water, balloons and kites, through dropping things, and through watching and cooking with fire, children get their first lessons about the natural world. They are also honing their labeling, classification, and ordination tools. In addition, they are learning, as yet unconsciously, that each of the elements serves many different functions. Classification tools teach children about sameness, while their ordination tools teach them about difference. Continual practice with classification and ordination, sameness and difference nourishes the child's attainment of syllogistic reasoning abilities.

If young children spend too much of their waking time with playing with chip-embedded toys or computers or watching television programs, they will have less time to interact with the elements and learn the lessons the elements have to teach. For the infant and young child, active involvement with the elements is the best preparation for the attainment of the tools of reason.

Plants and Animals

My daughter-in-law comes from El Salvador, where her parents have a farm. They raise chickens, among other animals and plants. So Norma decided she would raise chickens in her suburban Boston home. And she does. My granddaughter Lily has watched the chicks grow into adult chickens and has learned to collect the eggs from the nests. Earlier this summer, she called me with news that the eggs had hatched and that she had watched the chicks come out of their shells. When I visited a few weeks later, she came to me eagerly with one of the chicks to show me how big they had gotten in a few weeks.

When Lily comes to visit us on Cape Cod, she loves to go in the garden at the beginning of the season when we plant the vegetables. During the middle of the summer she loves to help pick the ripening strawberries, blueberries, and raspberries. (When the fruit was at its ripest, she asked, "Can I live here?") She watches the squash and pumpkins grow and helps us harvest them at the end of the summer; she has her pick of the pumpkins for her Halloween decorations. Watching the chickens hatch and grow and seeing the plants get bigger in the garden has helped Lily understand that one and the same animal or plant can get bigger—an appreciation that something can remain the same despite a change in its appearance. These are powerful learning experiences because Lily is actively involved in them, enjoys them, and is participating in them with loving parents and grandparents.

One of the ways I gauge the quality of a day care center or nursery school is the presence of well cared for plants and animals in the classroom. Not all children have the opportunities Lily has, but they can learn a great deal from what is in the classroom and what they observe in the world around them. "Why does a dog have a tail and I don't? How do ducks swim? What keeps them up in the water? What keeps birds in the sky? Why does a dog's tongue hang out of its mouth?"[5] When we remember that such questions are a form of mastery play, we can answer them in a way that makes sense to the child. To the tail question we might say, "Dogs don't talk so they have tails to tell us when they are happy or sad." This is really not wrong, just a syncretic/mythic way of looking at reality. What children will remember is not so much the answer as the fact that "a grown-up understood what I was asking."

The Cosmos

The sun, moon, stars, and planets intrigue young children and are the focus of much of their curiosity. Preschool children tend to think that the moon follows them when they go out for a walk. And they are curious about the sun and the stars as well. The following remarks were made by Russian preschool children: "Oh, the moon flew along when we went on the trolley and on the train. She too wanted to see the Caucasus." "I know how the stars are made. They make them from whatever is left over from the moon."

I knew a little boy who would question his mother about where the night went in the morning. Once, coming across a deep ditch with a dark bottom, he whispered, "Now I know where the night hides itself." And here is a reason for spring: "The winter got so cold it ran away, somewhere."[6]

In these examples the child has used his or her syncretic thinking to answer his or her own question. This, by the way, is a good strategy for dealing with a young child's questions. He or she really has an answer handy, and we need only turn the question back to the child and say, "What do you think?" Children, no less than adults, like to be asked for their opinions and are more than happy to respond to questions. Their answers will reveal, as do those above, that children construct their own syncretic views of the cosmos.

Playacting

Children's playacting is a direct descendant of therapeutic play, in which the child sees the imaginary child and the self as entirely separate. But in playacting, the child accepts the fact that she is playing a different role. Play becomes another way in which children further their understanding of rules and the concept that one thing can be two things at the same time. While my wife and I were having lunch at an outdoor restaurant, we observed a good example of playacting. A child at the next table got up, put a napkin on his arm, and approached his parents to take their order. He was not practicing to be a waiter anymore than a child playing doctor is practicing to be a doctor. The child has little or no awareness of what skills are required to be a waiter or doctor. In playacting, the child is taking the role with all the authority and prerogatives of the adult, and this is its true meaning. He understands that you can play at being an adult while remaining a child. As parents we should encourage and support this kind of healthy dramatic play. Here are some suggestions from gifted educator Ruth Almon for facilitating children's dramatic play.

Thus the playing of parts is very important, and it is up to us to support and to facilitate this. Let us accordingly always give something to our children or our grandchildren for their "theatre trunk" or "dressing up drawer." A discarded lace dress, an old top hat, a piece of beautiful red material for a royal cloak (or superhero cape), a piece of gold lamé, some cord and that old blue curtain, cast off costume jewelry—let us be ready at any time to cater for further props: a knight's breastplate can be made from old cardboard boxes with a stapler; a nurse's cap may be needed when the dolls have fallen ill, or even if one is allowed to take the odd thing to Father when he is ill—for a nurse such service is her *raison d'etre*, whereas a little daughter can become tired of it.[7]

Life Issues

Social roles are only one of the many aspects of the social world that elicit the young child's questions. Issues of birth and death, the human body, love, work, marriage, and sex are all of tremendous interest to young children. Asking children to answer their own questions is especially important when dealing with life issues, as they often use words that they do not understand or understand differently than we do. When one of my sons was seven, he came home from school and asked what "sex" meant. I started rummaging in my brain for some story about the birds and bees. Then I took my own advice and asked him what he thought. He said, "I don't know what it means, it just said at the top of my test paper, Sex F or M."

Young children are busy exploring and experimenting with the social world as well as the elements, plants, and animals, the cosmos. In these explorations and through their questions, children are creating their own learning experiences. They are strengthening their ideas about sameness and difference, growth and change. These experiences are essential to the development of reasoning tools. And in their richness, interest, and variety, they put television and computers to shame.

Building the Units of Math, Reading, and Science

When one of my sons was a preschooler, he came into my study one afternoon and announced that he could tell time. He is gifted mathematically, but telling time was precocious even for him. Thinking to call his bluff, I said, "That's great, Bobby, what time is it?" Without hesitation he answered, "4:30." I looked at my watch and indeed it was shortly after 4:30. I thought perhaps he had learned to dial the number on the phone to get the time and asked him if that was how he knew. "No, Dad, I can tell time." At that, he took my hand and walked me into our bedroom where we had a digital clock. "What time is it now?" I asked. "It's four, three, five," he answered, reading the numbers off the liquid crystal display.

This is a good example of how technology can make children seem more advanced than they really are. The difficulty of telling time from a clock face is the same difficulty that all measurement presents to young children. On a regular clock face, each number is both the same as every other number but also different from them. On a clock face the number three is like every other number on the clock face because it is a number. Yet it is also different from every other number in that it is the only number that comes after two and before four. Clock faces are particularly difficult because each number also stands for both hours and minutes. To complicate matters further, the "second" hand, for clocks that have them, is actually a "third" hand—in addition to the hour and minute hands. The digital clock bypasses all these difficulties by using spatial separation for the hours and minutes. To tell time from a digital clock, as Bobby did, you don't have to reason that one thing can be two; you only have to read the numbers from left to right. It is important to appreciate, however, that making a task easier does not make a child brighter. It was another couple of years before Bobby achieved the level of thinking in hour and minute units.

How Children Build Their Concept of Numbers

Like many other symbols, numbers have several levels of meaning. At the simplest level, a number can be used in the *nominal* sense as a name. A familiar example is the use of numbers to identify athletes. An athlete who wears the number 33, for example, does not have thirty-three of anything. A number used in this way is a convenient label for identifying a player during a game. At the next higher level, a number can used in an *ordinal* way to identify a position in a series. The score a child attains on an intelligence test, his IQ, for example, is an ordinal number. A child who attains an IQ score of 100 is not twice as bright as a child who attains an IQ of 50. There really are no units of intelligence, and intelligence test scores (like school grades) are simply rankings, not unit measurements. It is only at the highest level of *interval* numbers that numbers represent equal units and can be operated on arithmetically. A nickel, for example, is the multiple of 5 x 1 pennies and is also the quotient of a quarter divided by a nickel.

When young children build their concept of numbers they progress from nominal, to ordinal, to interval numbers. At the age of two or three, children will use a number in the nominal sense. When my granddaughter Lily was eighteen months old, she used numbers in this way. I held up two straws and asked her, "How many?" She replied, "Two." When, however, I held up three straws she again said "two." For Lily the symbol "two" simply stood for more than one and did not have an ordinal or interval meaning. As this illustration suggests, young children often use number words without understanding them in a quantitative sense.

By age three or four, many children have attained an understanding of ordinal numbers. This is greatly aided by engaging in classification and ordination play with blocks, and other size-graded toys that can be both grouped and ordered. An example is the colored plastic donuts that a child can arrange on a vertical stick from largest to smallest. They can also order a series of sticks of different lengths from shortest to longest. The child's ordinal understanding is only perceptual, however, and is based on visual differences. For example, if you ask a child at this stage to copy a "staircase" of size-graded sticks, the child can correctly copy the pattern. She does so by always choosing the next largest of the remaining sticks. If, however, you hand the child another stick of intermediate size that can be inserted into the completed staircase and ask her to put it into the series, the child is puzzled at the request. For the child at this stage the staircase is a finished perceptual pattern, not a set of elements arranged in order. Because the child sees a perceptual pattern, not a series of relations, she inserts the stick at random into the series without really understanding the problem.

It is only by the age of five, six, or seven, when the child has attained the age of reason, that she is able to construct interval numbers and arrive a true understanding of units. A true (or interval) unit is like every unit and different from it. The number three, to illustrate, is both like every other unit in that it is a number (its classification) but also different from every other number in its order of enumeration (its ordination). Three is the only number that comes after two and before four. Only after the child has constructed the concept of interval numbers can she really engage in arithmetic operations. The construction of interval numbers frees the child from the domination of perception. Now the child recognizes that six pennies spread out in a long row contains the same number as six pennies in a short row. Because the child grasps that the number of units is the same, she appreciates that what the long row gained in length, it lost in density and so the number remains the same.

The unit concept is basic to all quantification. All measurement requires units if it is to be truly quantitative and not just nominal or ordinal. Not all measurements are alike, however, and some are more difficult to construct than others. Time measurement is a case in point. Children first learn their birthdays in a nominal way. They can recite their birthday by heart, without really understanding the units of days, months, and years. Clock time also starts out in a nominal way. Six o'clock is just another name for dinnertime and eight o'clock is bedtime. Children are also beginning to get a sense of ordinal time, before and after, night and day, and the order of meals, breakfast, lunch, and dinner. Once children attain the age of reason, they can begin to construct interval time units.

As I suggested in the opening example, telling time from a clock face presents special problems. Each number stands for both hours and minutes. In mathematics, a similar difference—between ones and tens—is indicated by the ordinal position of the numbers, but this is not true for a clock face.

It usually takes children a year or two longer to learn interval clock time than it does to learn interval number in arithmetic. Liquid quantities, ounces, cups, and so on, also pose difficulties because the units are not visibly separate as they are with pennies or sticks. Understanding liquid units comes at the age of seven or eight as well. Units of weight pose an interesting problem. The child tends to think of weight as what touches the scale. If you put a long piece of wood on a scale so that it overlaps on each side, the child believes it weighs less than if the wood is cut into two pieces that fit completely on the scale at the same time. In the same way the child believes that she weighs more sitting down than standing up. The freeing of weight units from perception does not come until about the age of eight or nine.

It is hard to overestimate the importance of mastery play in attaining these different unit measurements. Only as the child experiments with classifying many different things, by color, size, pattern, and so on, does she develop the ability to classify, or the classification tool. Likewise only by ordering many different things according to size, or weight or time, does a child hone her ordination skills. With this play experience the child is ready, when maturation kicks in, to coordinate the classification (cardinal) and the ordination (ordinal) into a true unit concept that can be added, subtracted, multiplied, and divided. I believe that one of the reasons girls tend to do less well than boys (on the average) mathematically is that they are less likely to engage in manipulative play than are boys. It would be interesting to see if girls who were encouraged to engage in such play did better mathematically than those who did not.

How Children Build the Units of Literacy

The units of literacy follow the same developmental path as those of math, time, weight, and so on. Young children first learn the names of letters simply as names—nominal letters. They learn sight words like "stop" and "go" in the same way; they are names for a particular configuration of figures. The next stage of ordinality comes from children's being read to. When children hear a story several times they learn the order of the words, and want to hear them again and again. They are acutely sensitive to this order and get upset if it is not followed exactly. Supporting ordinal literacy is one of the reasons reading to young children is so important. It is a form of play in which the child is creating an inner ordering experience to coincide with the one he is listening to. Reading children poems and rhymes and teaching them songs adds to their understanding of verbal sequences. Reading to young children has many other benefits, including giving them the intuitive understanding that there is a connection between the printed and spoken word.

But it is not until children attain the age of reason that they can break the phonics code and understand that letters are in fact units. To truly appreciate phonics the child has to understand that one and the same letter can be sounded in different ways and that different letters are sounded in the same way. An example may help make this point. I was observing in a kindergarten classroom where the children were being taught phonics, an illustration of the current effort to push academics into kindergarten education. The teacher was working with a child who was having difficulty. He knew the short *a* and could correctly sound out "hat" and "cat" and "sat." But now the teacher confronted him with the word "ate." I could see the child's puzzlement and empathized with his frustration. He simply could not figure it out—he had not yet developed his reasoning tools.

I was troubled by another facet of this teaching moment. Before reaching the age of reason, children tend to think that adults are all-wise, all-knowing creatures who invented all things on this earth. Aware of this mode of thought, I had a sense of what was going on in this child's head: "I know 'hat' and 'cat' and 'sat,' but I don't know what this is. But this wise, all-knowing teacher tells me I should know this. But I can't figure it out. It must be me; I must be dumb!" When we try to teach children skills that require interval units before they have attained the age of reason, we run the risk of killing the child's motivation for learning, for schooling, and for respecting teachers. At this point I could not resist intervening and went over to the boy and said, "Mr. Rabbit tells me that when you get to be a little older, you will figure this out faster than you can say Jiminy Cricket."

Earlier I made the point that children's verbal facility often gave a false impression of their level of mental development. Language simply develops more rapidly than thought. The test I proposed was to ask the child to draw or to copy a diamond. This task requires the age of reason. In order to draw a diamond, the child has to understand vectors—the idea that one and the same line can move in two directions at the same time. This is the same issue we have seen over and over again as separating the child who has attained the age of reason from one who has not. In drawing a diamond the child has to make the line go down and out at the same time, and that is a problem for the presyllogistic child. Many highly verbal children have great trouble copying a diamond.

How Children Build the Units of Science

All science begins with observation. In many ways science develops through nominal, ordinal, and interval forms of conceptualization. Biology began with observation and classification of species. Darwin's observations led to the ordering of species from an evolutionary perspective. But it was only with Mendel's discovery of genes that biology had a unit—the gene—that could be measured. One could make a similar case for the other sciences such as chemistry, physics, and astronomy. Social sciences, like sociology, psychology, and economics, strive for interval unit measures but find these are hard to come by. I have already pointed out that intelligence test scores are ordinal not interval numbers. The same is true for SAT scores. We really should not use statistics on these scores, since statistics require interval unit scales.

My point is that children are best introduced to science in the way that science itself developed. Children are natural observers and classifiers. Each summer when my children were young, we took them with us to the two-week seminars I gave at a ranch in New Mexico. For the children there were many exciting activities. Ruth Clark, an anthropologist who was married to the ranch manager, took groups of children out to look for dinosaur bones. She told me that children are better than adults at finding such fossils, and my sons have a couple of bones and arrowheads to prove it. This idea has caught on. Today families can visit fossil digs that give the children an opportunity to exercise their powers of observation.

Because children have a natural talent for observing, naming, and ordering plants and animals, we should support and encourage this kind of play. The elementary school years are well spent in expanding on and elaborating children's observing and classifying talents. Experimentation—holding some variables constant while varying others—is best introduced after young people attain the second age of reason that comes with adolescence. Introducing experimentation too early, as with reading and math, can kill the child's interest and inclination to engage in science activities.

I know that this suggestion flies in the face of conventional wisdom. Particularly today when children work with high-level technology from an early age. But you really can't skip stages and this is as true for a science as it is for the individual. A case in point is psychology. The social sciences, including psychology, came late and only broke away from philosophy at the end of the nineteenth century. The early psychologists wanted to emulate their colleagues in the physical sciences and perform experiments. Because you can't run controlled experiments on humans, psychologists made the assumption that learning was the same in all species, and that studying learning in rats would tell about human learning. Psychologists spent almost a half a century studying rats, cats, and apes. Eventually psychology came to the realization that humans learn differently than mammals (we test hypotheses), and more than a half a century of research and theory was largely wasted. The exception is the work of psychologist B. F. Skinner, who discovered some learning principles that held across species. One of these was periodic reinforcement. If you are rewarded occasionally you will persist in activity longer than if you are rewarded each time or never at all. That is the principle behind slot machines and scratch cards.

It has always fascinated me that in a discipline that prides itself on experimentation and quantification, it is the observers and classifiers who are most cited in our textbooks. Sigmund Freud, Erik Erikson, and Jean Piaget were all astute observers, but their papers would never be published in our scientific journals. Yet they are the ones given the most space in our textbooks, and the ones most widely known outside the field. Psychology is still paying the price for its early infatuation with experimentation. If we encourage and support children's natural observation and classification powers, they will have a solid grounding to move into experimentation when they reach adolescence. Young people have a better chance of approaching science as a matter of play and love as well as work, when experimentation is not pushed too early. Science is a collaborative as well as a personal activity, and we will take up the contributions of play to social facilitation next.

seven

It Isn't Only a Game: The Role of Play in Becoming Social

Several years ago I traveled to Augusta, Georgia, to give a lecture to an education conference. I had been on the road for a number of days and took an afternoon nap at my host's house to rest up before my evening presentation. I was awakened an hour or so later by hushed children's voices outside my window. When I looked out, I saw several children playing hide-and-seek. They were whispering because they had been told the guest was napping. One child was saying, "Next time you can go as far as the tree." After a few moments, another said, "My turn; you can only go as far as the barn." These children were doing what children have been doing since time immemorial—playing a game of their own invention and making and breaking the rules as they go along. While playing these self-initiated games is fun, it also helps children learn the interpersonal skills needed to become effective social beings.

Games and Socialization

The period between early childhood and adolescence (roughly the ages from 6 to 7 to 11 to 12) is a relatively slow growth period between the earlier and later periods of rapid physical and psychological development. Growth during the elementary school years is gradual rather than abrupt. Physically children develop muscle strength and coordination a little at a time. By the age of eight years, for example, most girls can jump rope to a rhyme and do the hop, skip, and jump of hopscotch. By the same age both boys and girls can catch and throw a ball with some accuracy. Intellectually, however, even after children attain the age of reason, it will still be a couple of years before they fully appreciate that rules are manmade and not fixed and immutable. In middle childhood we see the same forms of play as we did in infancy and early childhood, but in a more elaborate, complex, and socially interconnected reincarnation.

In the mastery play of school-age children we see the same sequence observed at earlier age levels as repetitious practice gives way to innovative variations. Now, however, this play involves games with rules and rule innovation. At this age level, kinship play becomes a gender issue. Antipathy develops between boys and girls with an associated divergence in their play interests and activities. Playacting becomes less imitative, and school-age children often create their own clubs and secret play places. Therapeutic play is now social as well as individual. School-age children invent parodies and jokes that poke fun at the inconsistencies and absurdities of adult behavior. Individual therapeutic play is often a way of dealing with the challenges of growing up and creating a sense of selfhood. Before looking at these forms of play and games in particular, we'll consider a few general notes about the power of play at this age level.

Children's Games

Games Past and Present.   During middle childhood self-initiated play is not as dominant as it is during infancy and early childhood. School, organized team sports, and other extracurricular activities take up a considerable portion of the school-age child's waking hours. But self-initiated play remains an abiding disposition, and children engage in such play whenever they get the chance. Now that children have attained the age of reason, most of their play has progressed to games with rules. Many of these games date back hundreds of years. Games with rules include a wide variety of ball games, chasing games, circle games, mental games, sensing games, and strength games, as well as board games. Some games are *steady* (continuous over time), like cards and hide-and-seek, while others are *recurrent*, like marbles and jacks, which disappear and then reappear at a later time. Some games are *new*, created in response to new stories or films. The game of shark has been around as long as people have feared sharks. It was given fresh life by the popular film *Jaws*.

The way we play is that one person would be the shark and the rest of the people would be the minnows (the shark should wear goggles). The shark would stand in the middle of the pool and turn around and count to five while the minnows would start moving around the pool. As soon as the shark was done counting it would go under the water and start trying to tag the other players. The trick is the shark has to keep its eyes open under water but when it came up for air and had ten seconds and had to keep eyes closed while out of the water—or vice versa. Whoever gets tagged was the shark. The object is NOT to be the shark.

Here is a more complicated variant described on a game website:

The person who is the shark is up on the diving board on the end over the pool facing away from the pool. With at least two other people playing, who were the minnows, in the pool against the wall with the diving board. The minnows would pick a number (usually between 0 and 5). We usually hold up the number of fingers under the board so the person who was the shark would not hear. The shark would be quiet and look when he/she thought the minnows had started swimming for the other side. If the minnows were still touching the wall (feet count), the shark had to take a step down the diving board (away from the pool). The minnow would try and trick the shark as many times as the number they had picked. Each trick counted (taking a deep breath, splashing, kicking) if the shark looked or not. Once the specified number of tricks was done, all of the minnows would swim for their lives to the other side. Whoever got caught was eaten and came back as the next shark.[1]

Games and Social Institutions.   The many variations of the shark game speak to children's inventiveness and creativity of children. Games with rules, like the one described above, are the child's initiation into social institutions. Like other social institutions (e.g., the church), games retain a basic commonality despite their variations from generation to generation. Games such as jacks, tag, cards, and hopscotch date back centuries but are played somewhat differently today than they were in the past. Many contemporary games incorporate age-old rituals (turning a blindfolded child around three times before he begins chasing) and cues (telling a player she is getting "warm" when the player gets close and "cold" when the player is far off, and so on).

Games provide a set of rules that govern how to behave under certain circumstances. Like all social institutions, games exist only to the extent that there are individuals willing to participate in them. A church would cease to exist if it lost those who believe in what it stands for. In the same way, hide-and-seek would cease to exist if children didn't take satisfaction from playing it. Finally, for a social institution to survive, the members have to subordinate their personal needs and desires to the socially agreed on set of rules and rituals. This is as true for a church or synagogue ceremony as it is for a game of tag.

This point was emphasized by Swiss psychologist Jean Piaget as a result of his study of children's games: "It is through game playing, that is, through the give and take of negotiating plans, settling disagreements, making and enforcing rules, and keeping and making promises that children come to understand the social rules which make cooperation with others possible. As a consequence of this understanding, peer groups can be self governing and their members capable of autonomous, democratic and moral thinking."[2] Likewise, sociologist George Herbert Mead wrote that when playing games "children learn social responsibility, to relate to others and to integrate themselves within the social collective. In playing a game the child must be ready to take the attitude of everyone involved in the game."[3]

Adult Response (or Lack of It) to Children's Games.   Despite the importance of children's self-initiated games for socialization, adults often ignore them, their importance, and complexity. I recall how my sons and their friends were chased off a sledding hill by a neighbor who claimed the sleds were doing damage to his grass—buried beneath at least a foot of snow. When children play a pickup game of ball, a stray ball may hit a neighbor's window. Some adults object to children playing on the sidewalks and marking them up. And in the course of a chase or ball game, children may trespass on a neighbor's property. The following is perhaps an extreme example, but most of us can recall a neighbor who gave us a hard time when we were playing outdoors.

Inevitably, when we played a game in the street, our ball went into Miss Duncan's well-kept garden. She must have been waiting at the ready. For the minute the ball touched the ground, she dashed out through her little side gate, into her garden, snatched up the ball and in front of our very eyes, cut up the ball with big scissors.

In pairs, we drifted through an opening into the yard at the back of Miss Duncan's flat. We threaded a safety pin on a reel of black thread, fastened one end of the thread to a knob outside the spinster's window, reeled out the thread and spun it along until we were far away. Then we let the pin slide down the thread until it tapped on the window.[4]

As this recollection suggests, playing childhood games is not simply socialization in preparation for adulthood. It is equally (or more so) a desire for independence and a challenge to adult prerogatives of space and property.

The Pervasiveness of Children's Games.   Perhaps because we attend to children's games primarily when they cause us annoyance, we fail to see how common self-initiated games are to child life. But if we are open to looking for them, children's games are all about us. At the marina where I keep my little catboat, I see the children of the boating club members playing many different types of games. It is a family-oriented club and almost every pleasant afternoon or evening families share lunch or dinner while the children play. This often takes place in the area roped off for swimming. As I rig my boat, I can watch and listen to the jumping games (who can jump farthest from the dock) and the tag games as children chase one another in the water. This type of play, like many others, is truly spontaneous. You can see such play everywhere. One day as I left the supermarket, I saw a group of children playing a jumping game while waiting for their parents. They used the shopping carts as markers for how far they had jumped.

Although there are fewer spaces for contemporary children to play, they find them wherever they can. In front of the Boston public library on any given evening you can witness remarkable feats of skateboarding. These stunts are not haphazard and are rule regulated. The sidewalks of our suburban streets often bear the chalk marks of recently played hopscotch games. On some school playgrounds during recess children continue to engage in chase games, games of catch, and jump rope. And city children play pickup games of baseball or basketball if they can find a court or an empty lot.

Because there are few spaces and opportunities for children to engage in these self-initiated games, we Americans are losing our preeminence in our own national sport—baseball. Increasingly players from the Caribbean area and from Central and South America are the stars of our own baseball teams. Many of these players grew up playing for the fun of it and never participated on organized teams such as Little League. Again, learning is most powerful when it involves self-initiation and personal motivation. This is most likely to happen when young people play when they want to play, for how long they want to play and with whom they want to play. Despite more than 3 million children in Little League and numerous baseball camps, some of our best players are no longer homegrown.

Even without special places, children find a way to play a game. For my son Bobby's eighth birthday I took him and some of his friends to a movie. After the film, as we were leaving the theater, one of the boys took off to the station wagon parked at the corner and shouted over his shoulder, "Last one to the car is a rotten apple." My son, whom I have told thousands of times to tie his shoes, was tripping over his untied laces and had to stop and attend to his sneakers. As he did so, he raised his arm and shouted back, "Not included." The first boy, still running and without missing a beat, shouted in return, "No say backs." Even in this brief encounter game rules were laid down and there was even an (unsuccessful) attempt at negotiation.

Children's play in the confined spaces set aside for it by adults often differs from the play that goes on when children are in open spaces and free from adult supervision. Sociologists Iona and Peter Opie, who have done extensive research on children's games and the language and lore of children's play culture, put it this way:

We have noticed that when children are herded together in the play-ground, which is where the educationalists and the psychologists and the social scientists gather to observe them, their play is markedly more aggressive than when they are on the street or in wild places. They indulge in duels such as "Slappies," "knuckles" and "stinging," in which the pleasure, if not the purpose, is to dominate the other player and to inflict pain. In the playground it is impractical to en-gage in free ranging games such as "hide-and-seek" and "Relievo" and "kick the can." They are, as Stevenson said, the "well springs of romance and are natural to children in the wastelands."[5]

As children begin to develop their social skills through playing games with rules, parents come to play a less important part in their lives than they did during the early childhood years:

By age eight or nine a marked change appears in children's patterns of affiliation and loyalty. Parents are often distressed to find that their erstwhile loving child seems, during the third or fourth year of school, to have lost his affectionate and confiding nature and to become a stranger to his family. He may become as reticent as for-merly he was talkative, and seem only to live for the moment when he can tear from the house and join the other kids, leaving chores and lessons undone whenever possible. He may display an inso-lence, wholly at odds with his former good nature, and give the im-pression of laboring under a heavy secret.[6]

We can now look at how playing games with rules contributes to children's socialization as well as their capacity for innovation and in-vention, fantasy and imagination. As already noted, games with rules build on the earlier forms of play, namely, mastery, innovation, play-acting, kinship, and therapeutic. During infancy and early childhood these forms of play are largely individual and serve primarily to acquaint the child with the physical and social world. During middle childhood participating in games is equally (or more so) a means of winning peer group acceptance.

Starting the Game

Although many games are started on the spot, such as the one described above involving my son, many others have a prolonged starting process. Choosing sides, setting the rules, deciding who will be It can take a lot of time and may involve heated debate. There is first the matter of collecting the players who will participate in the game. One way is for two or three children to put their arms around one another and run across the playground summoning other children to join them in their game with some sort of rhyme or jingle:

> Pinch, punch, join in the ring
> Pinch, punch, no girls in.

The jingles change with time and place and so it is hard to give one that is immediately recognizable. But the principle is the same. Sometimes participation is involuntary if the children encircle an unfortunate soul who may be threatened if he does not join the group.

Many games center around who will be It. There are any number of ways to chose the It person, who is usually the chaser. One technique is to have the children who are playing stand in a circle. The chooser stands in the middle of the circle and, with eyes closed, turns slowly, stops, and points. Whoever is pointed at is It. In Japan, the child is chosen by drawing straws—a procedure sometimes used in this country as well. For some games, children feel that it is fairer if they are counted as two rather than as one. In one variant all potential players put out both fists when the chooser or "spudder" says, "Spuds up." He then taps each fist as he sings:

One potato, two potato, three potato, four.
Five potato, six potato, seven potato more.

As children learn to abide by the rules for choosing It, they learn to accept both the method of choice employed by the group and also the outcome, even if they are It. In this way children are learning to subordinate their personal wishes—not to be chosen It—to the rules of the game as decided by the group. As these illustrations make clear, a lot of socialization goes on even before the game begins.

Mastery Games

Age Changes in Rule Mastery

While the age of reason allows children to understand rules, the understanding they gain develops during the childhood years. Jean Piaget underlined this development in his study of children's marble games. He asked children from six to thirteen years about the rules of the marble game they were playing. Until eight or nine, children have a rather superstitious concept of rules. They assume that the rules were created a long time ago by adults and cannot be changed. At the same time, the youngest children Piaget studied had varied and inconsistent ideas about the rules of the game.

> It is only when they are at play that these same children succeed in understanding each other, either by copying the boy who seems to know more about it or, more frequently, by omitting any usage that might be disputed. In this way, they play a sort of simplified game. Children at the fourth stage (11–13), on the contrary, have thoroughly mastered their code and even take pride in judicial discussions, whether on principle or merely of procedure, which may at times arise out of points of dispute.[7]

Although younger children do not fully understand the rules of the game, they make believe they do in order to win social acceptance by the group. Older children, who have a better sense of themselves and greater self-confidence, are willing to argue about the rules and procedures.

Moral Rules Mastery

Children's mastery of rules through their games contributes to their understanding of moral rules. In his studies Piaget showed the relation between the rules children learned with marbles and those they understood with respect to morality. He argued that playing self-initiated games contributed to moral understanding. To study children's moral understanding in relation to their game play, he presented children at different ages with pairs of stories, each of which confronted the child with a moral dilemma.

Consider the following pair of stories. In the first story, a child who was helping his mother set the table tripped and broke three dishes. In the second story, a boy was trying to get some cookies he wasn't supposed to get and broke one dish in the process. After hearing both stories, the children were asked who was more to blame and who was to receive more severe punishment. Children under seven or eight said that the child who broke the most plates was the most to blame and should be punished more than the child who broke only one plate. Children who were eight or nine said that the child who broke the one dish doing what he was not supposed to do (breaking the rules) was more to blame. They also said that he should be punished more than the child who broke three dishes but did not break any rules.

On the basis of this research Piaget argued that children, thanks to play and maturation, moved from what he called *objective morality* to what he called *subjective morality*. Until the age of eight or nine, children believe that moral and immoral behavior should be judged objectively by the harm done by the act. After the age of ten or so, children judge moral behavior subjectively in terms of the person's intentions. During the elementary school years, then, children gradually begin to understand behavior in terms of motivation and intention, whereas earlier they evaluate behavior simply on the basis of its outcome.[8] As children master the rules of the game, they also grow in their depth of moral understanding.

In one of my studies we repeated Piaget's moral judgment work, but with a twist.[9] Prompted by a conversation with a lawyer, a friend observed, "That's all well and good when you are dealing with property damage. But what about personal injury?" So in our study we had children judge a child who had hurt another child on purpose (pushed him down to get him out of the way) with a child who had hurt another child by accident (slipped and gave him a bloody nose). We found that when it came to personal injury, children judged intention a year or two earlier than they did with property damage. Apparently children recognize motivation and intention earlier when it comes to hurting someone than when it comes to damaging property. Content can affect the way children make moral judgments.[10]

Verbal Rule Mastery

Another form of mastery play reflects the school-age child's comfort with language. Riddles are common during childhood, particularly among six- to-nine-year-olds, who are mastering language and playing with it. In riddles some words always have a double meaning. Much of the fun of riddles is the freedom they give children to break the rules governing word meaning. Consider the following:

What kind of shoes are made out of banana peels?
 Slippers.

Why did the tomato blush?
   Because it saw the salad dressing.

What do you call a fly without wings?
   A walk.

What do you say to spoiled lettuce?
   You should have your head examined.

What is small, red, and whispers?
   A hoarse radish.

How do you fix a broken tomato?
   With tomato paste.

In each of these riddles the answer is unexpected and involves a play
on words. Children usually ask these riddles in small groups. They must
have the same level of verbal skill to get the joke. In addition to being
amusing, riddles are establishing social hierarchies—those who are or
are not capable of understanding them. Many children who do not get
the riddle nonetheless laugh as if they do. They don't want to be ostra-
cized. Riddles are unique to the elementary school years and are an age-
related form of innovative language play. Although the majority of
riddles are passed down, many are invented by children themselves.

Aggression Mastery.   Another facet of rule mastery has to do with aggression, particularly rules regarding the use of aggressive words. As
children mature they learn to substitute verbal aggression for physical
aggression. But there are rules for the use of verbal aggression that
also have to be learned. This was illustrated in psychologist Gary
Fine's study of Little League players.[11] He found that there was a lot
of verbal aggression between the teams, for example, "Knock him

down if he gets in the way." "Smack his head in." If the language gets too hot and threatens to translate into action, some of boys usually step in to "cool their friends off." An interesting set of rules has to do with status and verbal aggression. The general rule is that a boy of lower status does not verbally attack a boy of higher status (usually determined by age). Here is an example from Fine's field notes:

> Tim, a ten-year-old utility outfielder for the Rangers, calls out to the opposing catcher, a twelve-year-old: "There's a monkey behind the plate." One of his older team mates (chastising him) shouts back, "He is a better player than you." Later in the game several of the older Rangers verbally attack Bruce, a low-status eleven-year-old, for criticizing their opponents.[12]

What is particularly interesting here is that even in the context of a game organized and coached by adults, preadolescent boys still set their own rules and social hierarchies. While participating in an organized team sport may inhibit these boys' ability to make and break the rules of the game, it does not stop them from making their own rules about the use of verbal aggression. In this connection one of the advantages of children's own games, such as hide-and-seek, kick the can, and hop-scotch, is that they are fairly simple. As a result, children can innovate with these games at an early age. One of the problems with having children in organized team sports such as football, baseball, or basketball is that it limits their ability to innovate, make and break the rules. But, as noted above, young people have a way of making and breaking their own rules even within the confines of highly organized adult games.

Mastering Cooperation and Competition

Two of the most important social skills that children learn through game play are socially acceptable forms of cooperation and competition. Children need to learn to balance their need to cooperate with other children in order to get things done with their need to compete in order to develop their sense of competence. While some children are more competitive or more cooperative than others, cooperation and competition are not fixed traits. Children have to learn how to appropriately adapt these social skills to the nature of the situation. Cooperation and competition are also heavily socially conditioned. In Japan, for example, the prevailing educational ideology is that the "the nail that sticks up, gets hammered down." In American society, in contrast, the ideology is that "the squeaking wheel gets the grease."

Despite these cultural overlays, children in any culture can learn healthy cooperation and competition through playing games. Adults can contribute to this learning by structuring the situation rather than structuring the activity. In a classic summer camp study investigators brought together two groups of eleven-year-old boys from similar backgrounds but complete strangers to one another to attend two separate summer camps in Oklahoma. To encourage each group to learn cooperation, the investigators confronted the boys with problems that they could only resolve by working together. For example, they provided the raw materials for the boys' dinner but left it up to the boys to decide how to prepare and serve it. By the end of the week both groups had become cohesive, decided on their leadership, and even chosen names for themselves—the Rattlers and the Eagles. This highlights the fact that, left to their own devices, young people can devise their own cooperative rules and hierarchies.

Until this point, neither group knew of the other's existence. After a week, the researchers told each group about the other. When they heard of the other group, both groups expressed a keen interest in competing with each other. The investigators accommodated this request by arranging a set of competitive games with prizes for the winners. The first game was a tug of war that the Eagles won. The Rattlers, in an effort to get even, burned an Eagle flag that had been left on the field of combat. As the competitive games continued, the hostility between the two groups increased to the point that the investigators felt they had to step in.

The researchers tried a number of different techniques to encourage greater social acceptance between the two groups. The first attempt, bringing the boys together for social events like meals and movies, ended in disaster. Rather than socialize, the boys used the occasion to continue their battle, with name-calling and food throwing. The next technique was more successful. The food truck bringing the ingredients for the evening meal was run into the mud on its way to the camp. The boys got together and used their tug-of-war skills to pull the truck out of the mud so that it could complete the drive to the campground. The boys then decided to prepare their meals together. After several other arranged incidents of this kind, boys from each group made friends with boys in the other group, and a sense of friendliness and camaraderie replaced the mood of antagonism and hostility.[13]

Both cooperation and competition involve rules. In cooperation the basic rule syllogism is: "I will help you and you will help me; I helped you, you help me." In competition the basic syllogistic rule is: "I will try and do better than you and you will try and do better than me: I tried to do better than you, you tried to do better than me." Both cooperation and competition are healthy. But competition can sometimes get out of hand, as in the above example. One solution to the cooperation/competition dilemma is to teach young people to compete with themselves and cooperate with others. In this way the child focuses on improving his own performance rather than besting another child.

Kinship Play

During middle childhood the criteria of kinship play change. For preschool children, proximity is the major factor in choice of playmates and playing with a member of the opposite sex is not stigmatized. In middle childhood, particularly after the age of seven or eight, kinship play becomes gender based. Boys are more interested in sports, fantasy games, and rough-and-tumble play. Girls are more interested in relationship building and intimacy. Girls are more likely to engage in dressing up, doll play, dance, art, and gymnastics. The earlier acceptance of cross-gender playmates is lost mainly as a result of the negative sanctions of a peer culture "characterized by acutely fierce ridicule, untempered by the gentility or politeness that comes to cloak most interactions in later life."[14] Mean-spirited teasing and derision replace the earlier chasing and kissing games between the sexes.

The need to distinguish oneself from the opposite sex is often expressed in verbal expressions such as "girls, ugh" or "boys, P.U." But in keeping with the rule orientation of this age-group, children devise elaborate rules about when it is okay to have any interaction with a member of the opposite sex. Here is one set:

Rule: The contact is accidental.

Example: You are not looking where you are going and you bump into a boy (or girl).

Rule: The contact is necessary.

Example: It is okay to say "pass the lemonade" to a boy (or a girl) as long as you don't show any interest in that person.

Rule: An adult insists that you have contact.

Example: "Go get the map from X and Y and bring it to me," when X and Y are of the opposite sex.

Rule: You are with someone of the same sex.

Example: Two girls may talk to two boys, but you have to stay physically far apart and not show any sign of interest in the opposite sex pair.

The pattern of in-group, out-group differentiation is not limited to boys and girls, and can happen within gender groups as well as between them. Both boys and girls make up rules about who can play with whom, within their age-group and sex. Being uncoordinated as a child, I had many experiences of not being welcomed onto the team. In my time, choosing up teams in gym class was done in the following way. Team leaders, usually exceptional athletes, were chosen by the gym teacher. The rest of us sat on the gym floor and waited as the leaders took turns choosing their teams. A heavyset kid and I were always left until last. When we did get chosen, we were always booed by the team we were supposed to join and jeered by our opponents. I never got to play much.

Children can be cruel, but this is often a matter of wanting to have a winning team rather than wanting to make me and the overweight kid feel bad. As kinship play devolves into groups separated by gender, ethnic, racial, and religious lines, as well as athletic skill, games can sometimes be used as vehicles of social ostracism and isolation. Social play is not always positive and can be hurtful to some children. But such play exposes children to what they can sometimes expect in the real world. These are the kinds of experiences children may never encounter when playing electronic games.

Playacting

In early childhood, playacting is largely imitative and helps the child appreciate that one thing can be two things at the same time. In middle childhood playacting, whether individual or group, serves a number of different functions. When school-age children play cops and robbers, or humans and aliens, they have to take the perspective of someone else. Because this type of play often has moral overtones—the bad guys against the good guys—this means that the child must be able to take the perspective of both hero and villain. This is true of many chase games as well and even the shark game described earlier. It is this ability to put yourself in another person's position, when it is different from your own, that George Herbert Mead regarded as the major socialization function of children's games, and particularly games or play in which children have to take different roles.

I became aware of another variety of playacting several years ago. A graduate student at Leslie University made an appointment to see me. When we met, Mark told me that he taught at a Montessori school nearby. He said that he was intrigued by something he had observed during the children's lunch hour. Both boys and girls would go into the woods and build makeshift "forts" out of tree limbs, rocks, and brush. Usually these forts were segregated by age and sex and involved a whole set of rules relating to the forts. Mark reviewed the literature and found that other investigators had observed and studied the same practices. He wanted to study the forts at his school for his master's thesis and asked if I would be his adviser. He had read some of my work and thought I would share his enthusiasm for the project.

I was indeed intrigued by the idea of forts because it was a facet of child life that I knew nothing about, despite many years in the field. I readily agreed to supervise Mark's research, which was a well-designed and significant piece of work. Mark visited the forts, took pictures of them, and interviewed the children. In addition, he corresponded with graduates of the school and asked about their memories of the fort experience. He also sent questionnaires to parents.

In compiling his results, Mark found that the fort culture was well established and had persisted for generations. Indeed, many parents recalled their own fort experiences at this school. He also found that the forts were highly gender segregated. The hierarchy of rules varied between the girl and boy forts. For girls, setting up rules of inclusion seemed all-important whereas such rules were of less interest to the boys. In terms of organization, the forts seemed to struggle between autocratic and democratic structures. Usually the autocratic took over when there was a strong leader, and the democratic when there was not.

A couple of the recollections of former participants give a sense of the importance these forts played in the lives of the students.

My fort gave me a sense of identity. . . . I was a tyrant in a world of willing servants. My main enjoyment of being in the fort was the sense that I was needed, and my authority was respected. Where I ran, they ran. My word was the final word.

As I bolted onto the field, passed the bell and gazed at the deep gully on the far side of the playground, I was transformed from just another student with average friends in a classroom, to Mel Gibson in *Braveheart*, raising a tempered spear as he charged into battle. (Alfie, 16, LMS alumnus from 1990 to 1997)[15]

I liked being in a fort because it gave me a sense of belonging to a small family, and it also gave me a purpose, namely, expanding and taking care of the fort. . . Fort play was a way for me to be comfortable expressing my opinions and leading other children at a time when I was very hesitant in front of adults. I think this made me a stronger person today. (Lorena, LMS alumna from 1991 to 1996)[16]

In many ways these findings duplicated those of an earlier study by psychologist David Sobel. Sobel interviewed twenty-eight English elementary school children in Devon, England, and thirty-eight elementary school children on Curaçao in the Grenadines. He asked the children to draw and to talk about their neighborhood, including the places that were special to them in some way. Of the children interviewed, 60 percent of the English children and 81 percent of the island boys and 75 percent of the island girls said they had built or played in forts.

The "dens" of Devon were most often hideaways in hollowed out hedges or overgrown thickets in the children's neighborhoods with secret entrances and emergency exit procedures in case of intruders. The children of Devon all showed proud ownership of their "rooms" and older children of ten or eleven especially valued places of private seclusion, and were especially protective of their clandestine privacy. In Curaçao the boys' "bush houses" and the girls' "playhouses" and "playshops" showed clearer gender differentiation, and a greater emphasis upon shared as opposed to private places, than was true for the Devon children.[17]

On the basis of his interviews and talks with children, Sobel concluded that these structures fulfilled a felt need by this age-group for privacy, independence, and self-sufficiency. It was the need to carve out a place for themselves in the world, either individually or in their peer group. Separation from family and teachers seemed important to these children; it gave them the space they needed to develop a sense of self. Sobel inferred that that these special places were like shelters for egos about to be born, an oasis before the turbulent years of adolescence with its painful, self-focused examinations. For Sobel, when children build forts, they experience themselves as shapers and makers of small worlds, which contributes to making them shapers of the larger world as adults.[18]

One is reminded here of children's tree houses and hideaways of all sorts. My oldest son remembered taking the large pillows off the couch to make a fort. He also recalled rolling huge snowballs (we lived in Rochester, New York, at the time, snow capital of the region) into forts that were used in snowball battles.

Children need their own space as well time for play. And in a variety of ways, children do create their own spaces—wherever they can—to give themselves some room, as well as some time, to grow.

Therapeutic Play

As children become social, they gain a sense of cohesiveness, of belonging to the society of children. Although they cannot rebel against
the sometimes arbitrary, often unjust adult world directly, they do so
indirectly. Mainly this is through parodies of what they have experienced at the hands of adults. Not surprisingly, school and teachers are
a popular target:

No more pencils, no more books,
No more teachers' dirty looks.

School is over, school is done,
We can stop learning and start having fun.

What did I learn? I can't remember.
And I'm not going to try till next September.

Our school is a good school, it's made of bricks and plaster.
The only thing wrong with it is the bald headmaster.

Therapeutic play in childhood can also serve individual growth
purposes. The therapeutic play of immigrant children serves many
different functions. Immigrant children must deal with a strange culture, an unfamiliar language, and often the fact of looking different
from other children. Some children must also cope with horrendous
memories. This was true for writer Loung Ung, who escaped from
Cambodia with her uncle and aunt but left her sister and brother behind. Loung had to adapt to her new life in Vermont while confronting the memories of seeing her parents killed and her baby sister
die. Loung gives one example of how play helped her deal with the
demons of her past:

I know that in my new home, there is no war, no hunger, or soldiers to be afraid of. Yet, in the quiet recesses of my mind, the Khmer Rouge lurks and hovers in dark alleys, waiting for me at the end of every corner. No matter how far I run, I cannot escape the dread that they have followed me to America.

To escape the soldiers, I sometimes find myself in a field far from our apartment. With my hair loose and free, I run through the elephant grass as tall as my thighs till I come to a brook. The sound of the gurgling water soothes and relaxes my mind, shutting out the thoughts of war. On the edge of the rushing stream stands a tree that reaches up high into the heavens with branches that dip toward the earth. I run and wrap my arms around the trunk, pressing my body against its hard bark. My eyes closed I imagine Chou [Loung's sister who remained in Cambodia] on the other side, her cheek smashed against the tree, her fingers reaching out for mine the way we used to when we were together. When I open my eyes, Chou is not there and my mind races to find her, wherever she is.[19]

Play enabled Loung to fantasize the happy moments she spent with her sister. These memories helped her counter the painful, frightening images of her past. The tree Loung used as a vehicle for her memories took on the qualities of a living person, offering her strength and protection.

When I worked for a family court in Colorado, I was involved in a case of a young teenage girl who had been abandoned by her parents; now she was caring for her two younger siblings on her own. Not having much food, she made them "bread" sandwiches without any filling. She used her imagination to cope with her hunger and her frustration at not being able to provide more for her younger brother and sister. Fortunately she and her siblings were taken in by family.

In childhood, therapeutic play serves both a social and a personal function. In their socially contrived and shared jeers, children share with peers a way of expressing anger and frustration at an all-powerful adult world. At the same time, the young person's individual imagination and fantasy can—as in the case of Loung and the abandoned girl—help her deal with the many demons of the past as well as the many challenges and anticipations of the future.

Self-initiated games with rules play an important role in children's growing sense of self and social awareness. While some of this can be gained through organized individual and team sports, much of it cannot. And as we have seen, children will find ways to make and break their own rules and will find spaces in which to grow despite adult efforts to constrain their spontaneity and creativity. In Part III we will look at ways that parents and teachers can support and encourage children's integration of play, love, and work. We will also look at the gifts play offers throughout the life cycle.

III The Power of Play

eight

Lighthearted Parenting

In *Anna Karenina,* Count Leo Tolstoy wrote that "all happy families resemble one another and all unhappy families are unhappy in their own way." I believe that all happy families resemble one another in that they have found ways to integrate play, love, and work in their everyday lives. That is what I mean by *lighthearted parenting*: parents make an ongoing effort to integrate play, love, and work into their child-rearing practices. They can accomplish this by using humor to socialize and to discipline, by sharing their passions, and by establishing patterns of family play, games, and experience sharing. Parents who use lighthearted techniques make child rearing easier and more fun, as well as more effective.

Humor and the Integration of Play, Love, and Work

The following story, told by psychologist Joseph Michelli, illustrates how parents can use a sense of humor to bring play, love, and work into everyday child rearing.

> Prior to leaving for an extended speaking tour, I told Andrew that I was concerned about his not being able to stay in his own bed. He

appeared to understand that he could help his mother, Nora, capture precious sleep if he would remain in his room at night while I was gone.

When I returned from my tour, Nora met me at the airport with Fiona in her arms. An exuberant Andrew raced down the corridor of the airport and yelled at the top of his lungs, "Great news Dad, no one slept with Mom while you were away!"

How would you have reacted in this moment? Would you have scolded Andrew? Looked around nervously at the people who might have heard his remark? Laughed hysterically? Tried to clarify his outburst to strangers? How do you explain to 200 people in a crowded airport terminal that it's not what they think?

Realizing that Andrew was dealing with change, and noticing his pride in managing that change made me laugh with unmitigated joy. I hugged him tightly and congratulated him on his success.[1]

Joseph Michelli was able to see the humor in this awkward situation, which allowed him to handle it in a supportive way. He did not worry about what other people thought. He was more concerned with reinforcing his son's feelings of achievement than with countering his own feelings of embarrassment. In putting his child's feelings first, Michelli avoided the *egocentric trap*. This trap, which all parents slip into on occasion, is looking at situations entirely from our own perspective and failing to take the child's point of view. Avoiding the trap made it possible for Michelli to laugh at the situation (play), express his affection for, and happiness with, Andrew (love), and engage in positive socialization of his son (work).

As this anecdote illustrates, the best defense against the egocentric trap is the ability to laugh at ourselves and at life's wry twists. Humor is a form of play because it always involves a new, unexpected experience. And that surprise, that sense of "aha," gets us to think outside of the box. Lighthearted parenting, more than just seeing the humor in situations, involves the active use of humor in parenting. When parents use humor with their children, it brings together play, love, and work. For example, when parents challenge children with riddles, they encourage thinking in new directions (play), reinforce family ties (love), and teach listening and language skills (work). Consider asking your school-age child the following riddles:

What did the broom say when it got tired?
   "I'm feeling sweepy."

What has four legs and goes tick tock?
   A watch dog.

Encouraging children to make up their own answers first increases the fun. The unexpected answers to these riddles encourage the child to imagine that a broom has feelings and can talk, and that a watch dog can go "tick tock." Taking the time and making the effort to give children riddles or other humorous challenges builds family bonds. In addition, imaginative challenges exercise the child's attentive listening and language comprehension skills.

Humor is most powerful if parents appreciate what makes children laugh at different stages of development. Sometimes what they think is funny may be lost on a child's immature mental development.

Ages and Stages of Humor

What makes children laugh is anything that goes against their expectations, such as a mole wearing sunglasses or a grown-up taking a pratfall. Their expectations are determined by their level of mental development. Puns, for example, are commonly derided as the lowest form of humor but they require the highest level of intellectual development. That is why adolescents read *Mad* magazine and why children like *Gulliver's Travels* as a story when they are children and as a satire when they are teens. Let's review the sorts of expectations children develop at successive stages of development, and how this knowledge can be used to introduce age-appropriate humor.

Infancy and Early Childhood

By the end of the first year, infants have attained object permanence. They can look for objects that they have seen being hidden from view. A one-year-old, for example, will expect to see a key ring that was hidden under a napkin when the napkin is removed. If the key ring is not there when the napkin is removed, the child will be surprised and bewildered but may not see it as funny. The world is too new and the child's grasp of it still too tenuous for her to enjoy failures of expectations. Infants smile to express happiness, but true laughter does not occur until early childhood.

At the age of two or three, children have developed a number of expectations that parents can use to encourage laughter. For example, preschoolers expect to see us and hear us in the way in which we customarily present ourselves. But if we put on a funny hat or change our voice when we are reading a story, these are unexpected and the child finds them funny. During a visit to our home, my two-year-old great-niece kept trying to feed our dog, Remy, with bits of her lunch. Using my roughest voice and making an ogre face, I said, "The ogre says don't feed the dog." She made a funny face and stopped. When we visited her at Christmas, she made a stern face and said, in her own ogre voice, "The ogre says don't feed the dog," and giggled. Similarly, when my two-year-old granddaughter Heather put her finger in her nose, I made a disgusted face and said, "Gross." Now when we visit her, she teases me by putting her finger to her nose and waiting for my reaction. It has become a game we play. Of course both these children were familiar with the way I change my voice and make faces when I read stories to them, and to my silly jokes. I would not have employed these techniques if the ground had not been prepared for their use.

Children of this age are also beginning to understand space and size relations. They laugh when they see a dozen clowns come out of a Volkswagen at the circus. They know the small car cannot possibly hold that many clowns and so they laugh when it does. Young children are also accustomed to adults being physically coordinated. So when they see a clown fall down, this is funny because it is unexpected. Someone who trips, without being hurt, is funny. Falling down is not what grown-ups do; it is a surprise. The child's rapidly developing language skills provide another avenue for humor. Children find nonsense words funny because they are nonstandard English and thus are unexpected. With my preschool granddaughters Lily and Heather, I play a "changing the name game." I ask them if we can call a chair a "clop," and they laugh and say no. "Can we call it a gobbledee gook?" "No," with giggles again.

Dr. Seuss understood this kind of humor and incorporated a lot of nonsense words into his stories, which contributes to their fun. With young children we must be careful about the words we use. If young children learn a swear word they will use it to get a rise out of us, even if they have no idea what the word means. If we can keep a straight face, we can say, "I don't like to hear that word." We also have to be careful with names. Children are very protective of their names and don't want to be called by anything else, except perhaps a nickname that everyone uses. In preschool, for example, some children like to be called by their full name just in case there might be another Walter or Judy in the class. Also, young children believe that if they are called a name, they have the trait the name implies. Young children are very hurt when they are called bad names. It is only when they reach the age of reason that they can recite, "Sticks and stones will break my bones, but names will never hurt me." Nonetheless, bad names never stop hurting.

Childhood Humor

Once children reach the age of reason, they expect propositions to be logical. Riddles are funny because they fail to meet the child's logical expectations. Consider the following riddles:

What did one potato chip say to another?
  Would you like to take a dip?

Why was the belt arrested?
  For holding up the pants.

What do you call a funny book about eggs?
  A yolk book.

The answer to each riddle is in a way illogical and thus foils the child's expectation of a logical answer. Riddles are funny for just that reason. Moreover, they encourage imaginative thinking that diverges from the norm. With this age-group it is often fun to start off the day with a riddle (you can find many on the Web or in books) and challenge your child to come up with an answer by dinnertime.

The kinds of pratfalls and costumes that make young children laugh seem babyish to older children. Indeed school-age children often use humor as a sign of their new maturity. When they don't laugh at what little ones laugh at, this shows that they are more grown up than their younger siblings. We see the same age difference with respect to children's reaction to magic. While preschoolers are awed by magic tricks, older children are not. They know that rabbits and pigeons do not come out of hats, and that you can't saw people in half. The attraction and fun of magic at this age is a fascination with how these tricks are done. Some children become quite adept at performing magic tricks and use them to amaze their younger siblings. It is another marker of their growing maturity.

School-age children can be cruel and may use derogatory jokes, names, and rhymes to embarrass and hurt another child's feelings. In using humor with this age-group, be careful not to use humor in a derogatory way. Children do as we do, but they also do as we say. And if we make jokes about people with disabilities or about people of other races or religions, our children learn that this is okay and are inclined to do likewise. Humor, like so many other good things in life, can be misused. And when it is, it loses its positive benefits.

Discipline with Humor

When my oldest son was twelve, we left him alone for a few hours while we were running errands. His only chore was to let the dog out in the yard for his afternoon run and relief. When we got back, Paul was deeply engrossed in a book he was reading and had forgotten to let the dog out. We knew that as soon as we noticed that the dog had done his business on our new rug. I was really angry and was ready to chew Paul out, but my wife counseled patience. For some reason, perhaps because of my wife's intervention, I thought of the Ralph Kramden character in a popular TV program, *The Honeymooners*. When Ralph got angry at his wife he would pound his fist into the palm of his other hand and say, "To the moon, Alice!" So I punched my fist into the palm of my hand and said to my son, "To the moon, Paul." In this way I was able to express my anger without putting my son down or attacking his character or his personality.

Our children can make us angry, sometimes vehemently so. Sometimes they do this on purpose and sometimes inadvertently. Most of us learn how to handle anger from our own parents. Some of us were smacked when we got out of line; others were never hit but were shamed instead. If we were lucky, our parents handled discipline with humor. When we discipline lightheartedly, we accomplish three important goals. First, we manage our own negative feelings in a positive and constructive way. Second, we provide our children an effective and constructive way of handling their own emotions. Third, we provide a healthy model of parenting for our children to use when they themselves have children. We have to remember that while our children's unacceptable behavior is short lived, how we handle that behavior has long lasting consequences.

One of the ways young children anger parents is throwing a tantrum in a public place, which embarrasses their parents and annoys bystanders. Psychologist Joseph Michelli tells of one creative mother who made signs that she took with her when she went shopping with her son. One of the signs read, "PLEASE EXCUSE HIS TANTRUM" and another read, "DANGER: MOOD UNDER REPAIR." These signs made the passersby laugh and pay less attention to the tantrum. The boy gave up his behavior. He wanted to call attention to himself, but not as an object of humor.[2]

Michelli also tells a story about himself and his young son Andrew who was having a very bad day:

Everything I asked him to do, was met with a parent's favorite response, "No." Timeouts were getting us nowhere. He was out of control, and I was quickly joining him. As my blood pressure rose, my temper shortened and my voice became more intense. I asked myself where did this child come from and can I take him back without a receipt? It is said that change comes from either inspiration or desperation. My despair caused me to disengage from the morning-long warfare. I walked into his room waving a white flag and requesting peace.

Andrew began laughing and asked if I would read him a story. As he sat on my lap, I noticed he was feverish. As it turned out he had been feeling ill the entire morning. The same child who appeared to be my enemy just moments before, was now lying quietly and contentedly in my arms.[3]

Comedian Bill Cosby gives other examples of using humor to discipline, and how children can learn to use it in return.

One day a friend of mine down the street said to his eight-year-old son, "Sam, you do that again and I'll tear off your arm and beat you senseless with it." Sam responded by laughing, for he knew the threat made more sense coming from a grisly bear than from his father. Laughter is not the ideal climate for a disciplinarian.

Especially when the disciplinarian is doing the laughing. My daughters, for example, have always known that whenever I scolded them I was miscast and could easily be bumped from the role.

"Young lady," I sternly said to one of my daughters one night, "I never want to see you doing that again." "Then don't look," she said and we both laughed. No student of children from Dr. Freud to Dr. Seuss has been ever able to meet the ultimate challenge. How do you handle the child that first breaks up the living room and then you?[4]

Other writers have acknowledged the power of discipline with humor. Famed English psychologist Susan Isaacs gave the following example.

Helene, the mother of two boys eleven and three, has found humor a good way to sidestep unnecessary confrontations. She remembers one morning when Shelly, her three–year-old, was grouchy and she could easily have had an argument with him. She started looking around the room as if she had lost something. "I wish that happy Shelly would come back," she said "Where is he?" Shelly couldn't help but respond. Humor can help us transcend the negative emotions associated with conflicts.[5]

In his book *Proud Parenthood*, John Felix gives yet another illustration of discipline with humor:

The refusal of a four-year-old-child to go out of doors can be exasperating. You might recognize your beginning anger and grab the child's coat with the same vigor that you are tempted to grab his throat. Holding up a sleeve, you might say, "Let's see now, your leg must go in here somewhere." There's no guarantee, of course, that such an approach will get the child dressed more quickly. But it will help minimize your frustration.

If you find yourself starting to boil every time you pass your son's incredibly cluttered room, it might help to keep the door shut. Or you might simply resolve again to be calm as you hand him the rake and tell him to get busy cleaning it up.

Hopeless disorder seems to be the universal characteristic of boys' rooms.

"Mom, my right shoe is lost."

"That's ridiculous. How could it be lost? Just stop and think; where did you take it off last night?"

"In my room."

"It's lost."[6]

When we discipline with humor, we often use contrary-to-fact propositions (using a rake to clean up a room) and irony (it's truly lost!), which encourage imaginative and creative thinking.

Let me give you a personal example of how disciplining with humor can rub off on children we teach as well as those we are trying to rear. For a number of years I ran a school for what I called "curriculum-disabled children."[7] These were children of average or better ability who were functioning below the academic norm. Many of these children suffered from a mismatch between their learning styles and those demanded by the schools. My undergraduate students tutored these children and helped them learn strategies for coping with the school curriculum. After a year or two, most of the children were ready to return to the public school system and perform at their ability level.

One of the children in the school, Ron, was a bright young man but quick to anger. One day, when another child knocked over his toothpick sculpture, he picked up one of the child-size chairs and charged at the offending youngster. I intervened, put my arms around him and the chair, and said, "Shall we dance?" Ron had to smile, although now he was angry at me for grabbing him and stopping his attack. After we put down the chair I said, "It is okay to get angry, but we have to use words to tell people we are angry at them, not hit them with things." A few days later I stopped by Ron's desk and said, "Ron, I have some good news for you: I have to go to the dentist." Without raising his head, he replied, "I hope you have a thousand cavities." Ron had learned how to express his anger with words.

A common discipline problem stems from our need to set limits. There is such a thing as watching too much television or eating too much junk food or playing computer games for too long. Children do not always know or do what is best for them. That is what parents are for. Deep down, children want and need limits. They need to feel that they are living in a world that is under control, and in setting limits we give them that reassurance. One strategy is to create the rules and limits with your child or children. When we do this, we can jointly set the consequences of breaking the rules. If we want to bring humor into the equation, we can make some of the punishments funny. "If you track mud into the house again you are going to have to wear a MUDTRACKER sweatshirt for a week." "If you don't make your bed, you had better find something to make me laugh, and laugh hard."

In setting limits with humor, we put our children's behavior in perspective. It is not the end of the world if a child tracks mud into the house or doesn't make his bed. The problem is that we sometimes blow these issues way out of proportion, making the problem worse rather than better. We lose control of our emotions and our children do likewise, producing bad feelings all around.

On the other hand, if we deal with limit setting in a lighthearted way, our children are more likely to relax and learn the rules. Humor helps us remember what is really important—we have a healthy, normal child who, like all children, makes her parents crazy.

In using humor as a disciplinary technique, we are bringing play, love, and work into our parenting. The joke or humor is the play part; the deep affection that is our reason for using humor is the love part. And the social learning, which is the outcome, is the work part. The best reason for using humor as a disciplinary technique is that it is both effective and rewarding.

Sharing Our Passions

One of the best ways of ensuring that our children both play and develop lifelong habits of play is to share our personal passions with them. Our passions are activities we love and engage in whenever we have the opportunity to do so. Whether golf, gardening, fishing, or jogging, passions give us a creative outlet that we may not find in our jobs or professions. They allow us to realize our personal talents and abilities. Children are blessed when we have passions that we can share with them. While they may not take them up, they have the opportunity to see us engaged in something we love and do for no other reason than the sheer pleasure of doing it.

I have a good friend and colleague who has a passion for baseball. He follows the teams religiously, goes to the ballpark whenever he can, and coaches a Little League team. He has conveyed this passion to his son, who has developed an equally strong love for the game. Father and son play catch in the yard and go to baseball games together. In sharing his passion with his son, my friend has created an abiding common interest that will continue long after his son leaves home. Sharing a passion differs from paying for music or sports lessons, when you have little interest in these activities yourself. If our children see that we really love something, they are much more likely to take it seriously than if we take them for lessons in which we have little or no interest.

A personal story illustrates how sharing a passion can provide life-long bonds. When my sons were growing up, I was teaching at the University of Rochester. We bought a small cottage at a nearby lake where my wife and sons spent the summer, and I commuted daily. I love water sports, swimming, and boating, and I was fortunate to be able to share those passions with my sons at the lake. They are grown now and still share my love of water sports. One of our greatest pleasures, even today when they have their own families, is to sail together on Cape Cod Bay in my little catboat. It is deeply gratifying for me to see my sons take the helm with such confidence and assurance.

Like it or not, many of the passions parents share with their children are sex linked. While fathers can and do share their love of baseball or water sports with their daughters, it happens less often. Although women have made important inroads into professional sports, many sports remain male dominated. And there are still strong social prejudices surrounding appropriate male and female activities. In our society, it is okay for girls to engage in what are usually regarded as male activities. It is less acceptable for boys to share their mothers' passions when they are regarded as feminine pursuits. Sewing, needlepoint, and ballet come to mind. Cooking is one of the few unisex activities, but males are more likely to cook on the grill than in the kitchen. These social biases are hard to overcome unless we make a special effort to do so.

It is best when the whole family shares a passion such as skiing, sailing, or biking. Each child is brought into the sport at an early age, and it becomes a family affair. I have no objection to a young child being taught to ski, skate, or swim, as long as the whole family engages in this activity. Such a shared passion bonds the family over the years and brings far-flung family members together. Nonetheless, even when one parent shares a passion it is still valuable for the children to have this experience. Although my wife does not share my passion for sailing, she has generously supported my sharing this love with our sons.

Sharing by Example

Sometimes we do not need to share our passions directly; just the fact of engaging in them can be a powerful learning experience. This kind of modeling was common to the experience of many individuals who attained eminence before age forty. In a study of 120 people with a variety of artistic talents, one of the findings was that "about one-third of the sculptors has an adult role model for art activities. A parent or relative enjoyed sketching occasionally, or was learning to do water colors, or make pottery."

The sculptors had recollections such as the following: "I grew up in a house that was full of painting and music. From the time I was little, I was involved in one of those things, either watching it or playing around with it or whatever. It was something that father did; it wasn't for the benefit of anyone else. So I got to experience it as the way somebody spent their time. A lot of people don't get to do that. . . . it just seemed natural to me."[8]

The idea that these parental pursuits were just something that adults did for their own pleasure and enjoyment, rather than because they were obliged to do so, is crucial for encouraging playfulness. It was equally present in the lives of those who became successful pianists. One pianist recalls "plunking on the keys as much with the palms of my hands as with my fingers, and running to my mother and saying, 'Was that a nice song,' and going back and doing it again."

The pianist's parents encouraged their children to sing songs, identify notes, or pick out tunes. Some parents played children's records, others kept the radio tuned to a FM classical music station. Much attention, praise and applause was given to the child's musical efforts. When the children developed skill, they played duets with their parents and entertained family and friends who came to visit. In the early years, music was an amusement for the parents and the child. It was an interest parents could share with their child and an opportunity for parents and children to play together and feel a closeness with one another.[9]

Sharing our passions, even by example, is far different from teaching children academic skills or giving them lessons. It amounts to revealing ourselves as people, the things we love to do when we have free time. When we share or model our passions, we free our children to engage in activities they are not obliged to perform (play). In addition, sharing passions builds strong family bonds (love) and teaches socially valuable skills (work). Sharing our passions with our children is yet another way in which we can bring play, love, and work together in our parenting.

Sharing passions is not limited to parents. I often suggest to teachers that they share their passions with their students. When teachers do this, they present themselves in a different light. Teachers who share their passions display an excitement and enthusiasm they may fail to show for a rigid curriculum that gives them little opportunity for innovation. When teachers are enthusiastic about a subject, children get the idea that learning can be exciting. Teaching, like parenting, is most effective and most pleasurable when the instructor shares his passions with the students.

Children's Passions

Throughout this book I have emphasized the importance of individual differences. Some children have their own passions from an early age. This is particularly true of gifted children. When parents support these passions, as in the examples above, the children go on to realize their full potential. Other parents may not support their children's passions, not out of spite but out of concern for the child's future success in life. Some children give in to parental pressure, but others harden their determination. A case in point is Maria Montessori:

> There was a certain note of authority to her personality. In games with other children she was usually the leader. Playmates sometimes objected to the contemptuous way she could treat them. She had a strong, somewhat flippant way about her. Those she disapproved of she dismissed with a phrase like, "You, you aren't even here yet." Or, "please remind me that I have made up my mind never to speak to you again." She held her own with adults too. When a teacher objected to an expression in "those eyes," Maria responded by never raising her eyes in the teacher's presence again.[10]

As a young woman, Maria insisted on going to medical school over the protests of her family and society in general. She was the first Italian woman ever admitted to medical school. The faculty did not make it easy for her. Because she was was not permitted to look at naked cadavers alongside men, she had to dissect her cadavers alone at night. Nonetheless she persisted and ended up valedictorian of her graduating class. Parental opposition drives some young people to realize their ambitions and talents.

Some children will follow their parents' lead and share their passions over a lifetime. Others will find their own way despite parental opposition. In a study of children who have attained eminence before age forty, researchers concluded that what seems universal in people who have excelled in their chosen profession is that they felt an "underlying, *love, respect and honesty* from their families."[11] Those character traits seem to be the critical common elements that run through the family histories of those who have attained eminence in society. But they are also the character traits of parents who have children who become happy and successful and productive in all walks of life.

Family Time

In my book *Ties That Stress*, I describe changes that have taken place in the American family since the middle of the twentieth century.[12] The pre-World War II nuclear family was characterized by romantic love, maternal love and domesticity, and the value of togetherness. Romantic love was the belief that there is only one person in the whole world for you, and when you meet that person, you will fall in love, marry, and live happily ever after. Maternal love was the belief that women have a maternal instinct to take care of their children, to stay home and rear them. Domesticity was the belief that the home is the center of family life, in the words of writer Christopher Lasch, "a Haven in a Heartless World."[13] Togetherness was the value that the family comes first and precedes individual needs, interests, and activities. Dinnertime, for example, took precedence over all other obligations and activities.

The postmodern permeable family is characterized by the sentiments of consensual love, shared parenting, urbanity, and the value of autonomy. Consensual love is the understanding that love is a mutual agreement between equals that need not be permanent. The prenuptial agreement epitomizes the sentiment of consensual love. Shared parenting is the belief that fathers, relatives, and nonparental caregivers can help rear children. Today some 63 percent of children under the age of five are in one or another form of child care. In the prewar era it was at most 10 to 20 percent. Urbanity has come with television and more recently the Internet, which has brought the external world into the family and made its boundaries more open and permeable than was true for the nuclear family.

Finally, the value of autonomy means that individual needs, interests, and activities can take precedence over those of the family. Shared family meals are the exception today. For example, the number of meals purchased at a restaurant and eaten in the car has increased from nineteen meals per person in 1985 to thirty-two meals per person today.[14]

Most families today are probably some amalgam of nuclear and permeable sentiments and values. Nonetheless, it is a fact that shared family time has diminished from what it was in the past. And middle-income parents spend much of their shared family time driving their children to lessons, play dates, and soccer and Little League games. There is not much time for relaxed family interaction. Yet shared family time is essential for family cohesion as well as for the family's physical and mental health. I was impressed when one of my undergraduate students told me that he vacations with his parents and sister. He is one my best students, takes the initiative in research projects, participates in community service, and plays on a Tufts sports team. The family is really tight, which I have to believe has contributed to the many positive qualities he displays.

Making Time for the Family

It is difficult in our hurried and hurrying society to find time to reserve exclusively for the family, but it can be done. An Israeli colleague who has made major contributions to the assessment and education of children with special needs described how he does this. From Friday to Saturday evening he celebrates the Sabbath with his family. Work-a-day intrusions are not allowed as the phone is turned off. No one drives the car or runs errands, discusses work topics, or the like. Few of us today have the luxury (or the discipline) to take a day off to spend with family. Given the multiple demands on our time, even having dinner as a family every evening is often not in the cards. Nonetheless, there are things we can do that can further family togetherness and cohesion. I have already described the importance of encouraging laughter, using humor in discipline, and sharing passions. Even though we don't set aside a particular time for these activities, they nonetheless serve the same purpose.

In addition to these everyday lighthearted parenting practices, it is still valuable to set aside some time, say, once a week (not necessarily the same time or day), that is reserved for the family. This can be time spent going for walks or bike rides, playing a game, having a meal, or telling stories. But the time should be made sacred and put above all else. Sometimes we may have to give up a meeting, a game, a concert, or even a trip to be there for family time. When we make a sacrifice, when we give up something that is important to us in order to be with our children, we give them something that is invaluable—the assurance that they are important in our lives and that we care about them deeply. If children are secure in this feeling, we have given them the best preparation we can to cope with anything life throw at them later.

From an early age, I played cards with my sons on a regular basis at least once a week. My wife did not play but was an active kibitzer. When the boys were small we played simple games like War. In playing with little ones it is important not to be impatient. Playing games is new for them and they need to take their time. The older boys had to be cautioned not to pressure their younger sibling to make his moves. We should also let children make mistakes in their play and learn from them. I sometimes let them win; they knew this, but they still enjoyed winning. As they grew older the games got more complicated. We began to play Hearts and Gin Rummy. As adolescents *they* sometimes let *me* win. We still play card games when we are together.

Riding in a limousine to my middle son's bachelor party, we played cards all the way to the restaurant.

There are a wide variety of family games that can be enjoyed by all. One of our favorites is Fictionary, which we play on holidays or during storms. Using the Oxford standard dictionary, each player looks through the dictionary to find a word that the other players are unlikely to know. He or she then says and spells the word and all the players have to write their own definitions. When all the definitions are written, each player reads his or her idea of what the word means. The players then vote on whose definition is most likely to be true. The player who gets the most votes, even if it is not the correct definition, wins that particular round. The dictionary is then handed over to the next player and the game is repeated. It really challenges the imagination and can be quite funny.

Games like Fictionary are for people who like words. Other families enjoy action or sports games like softball or touch football. Some families may favor going on outings to a park, museum, or ball game. If children and parents do not take pleasure from the same things, it is important to find at least one activity everyone can share. We all have to eat, so one activity could be to have each member or the family, or pairs of family members, prepare the meal for the special family time. Another option is to rotate who chooses the activity for family time. This means that every family member has to subordinate his or her likes to that of the other members. This is a healthy way for families to understand and appreciate what other family members enjoy in their leisure time.

Shared Experience

In colonial times, families met together each day to read the Bible. It has been estimated that by the time a young Puritan reached puberty, he or she had read the Bible sixteen times.[15] For religious people, reading the Bible or other religious books may be a meaningful family activity. Other families talk about a book, article, or story. We are a story-loving species, and using family time to tell interesting tales is attractive to all. For example, children love to hear about their parents' childhoods, particularly if they grew up in a different place and in different circumstances than their own. They also like to hear about relatives, near or distant, who have done interesting things. Because extended families are so scattered, telling our children stories about their distant relatives often fascinates them.

Family time can also be used to develop a habit of sharing everyday experiences. This sharing can pay big dividends when children get older and communication becomes more difficult. If patterns of sharing experiences are developed early, they are likely to carry through into adolescence. One way to start children sharing their experiences is by first sharing our own. We might begin by saying, "My happiest memory of the week was when my students said they really liked my Erikson lecture. What was your happiest memory of the week?" We can prime this discussion pump with similar questions. "When I was going to school, my favorite teacher was Mrs. Robin; she liked the things I wrote and encouraged me to write more. Who is your favorite teacher?" We need to use questions that are fun to answer and do not put the child on the spot, as in, "What grandparent do you like best?" Children are much more willing to talk about themselves and their experiences if we begin by sharing our own. In this way it becomes a true discussion and not an interrogation. Sharing experiences has other benefits, over and above building positive habits of communication. John Dewey wrote that learning is the "representation of experience."[16] He felt that raw experience itself does not teach; we only learn from it when we represent it in some way. Talking about our experiences is one of the ways that we represent them and make them our own. That is why teaching is such a powerful learning activity. We have to make the material our own before we can convey it meaningfully to others. When we set aside a time for children to talk about their experiences, to put them into words, it helps them make these experiences personally meaningful. Talking about their experiences gives children a richer sense of who and what they are. In turn, as we listen to our children talk about their experience, we get a deeper insight into their everyday lives.

In sharing experiences, we have to be thoughtful about children's ages and stages. Obviously children's ability to share their experiences changes with age. Here are examples of children's retelling of their experiences at different age levels when they were asked to recall their best memories.

Five-year-old: "My best memory was when Grandpa was in the war. He dropped torpedoes on ships."

Seven-year-old: "I remember when I was at camp and Nick, my best friend, came over to my house for the night and we had lots of fun. I liked it a lot."

Nine-year-old: "I remember when I was in my cousin Margo's wedding and I was a flower girl. It was a lot of fun. I wore a white dress with a pink sash. I had a white headband with little flowers and bows on it."[17]

The first memory reflects the thought processes of a child who has not yet reached the age of reason and has not yet arrived at categorical thinking. The child of this age organizes her experience in terms of the most striking features of events without worrying about details of time and place. By age seven the child begins to organize memories in a logical sequence and adds personal reflections. The memory of the nine-year-old is not only sequential but is filled with a lot of descriptive detail. Recall memory at each age level reflects the child's level of thinking ability as well as the events that are most important to that particular developmental stage. It is important to listen attentively to what our children say, even if it seems dull and uninteresting. When we make an effort to really listen, we begin to see the world from the child's point of view. In so doing we show respect for the child's communication and reinforce his desire to share future experiences.

Sharing experiences—whether about our childhood or about likes and dislikes, happy and unhappy times—is another way of integrating play, love, and work. For when we share experiences, we represent our experience (play), share it with our family (love), and develop communication skills (work). It has another benefit as well. Earlier I suggested that making sacrifices for our children gives them a sense that they are important in our lives and that we care about them deeply. This gives them roots, a sense of being well grounded that enables them to withstand some of life's strongest winds. When we share experiences with our children, we come to appreciate them as individuals and give them the freedom to be the best that they can be. We give them wings to sail with the wind. With roots and wings, children are best prepared to weather the climate of schooling we will talk about next.

nine

Schooling with Heart, Mind, and Body

Formerly clear boundaries between home, school, and the world at large are now permeable and open. Elementary school students are text messaging under their desks, maintaining their own blogs, and participating actively in one or another online community. Whereas in the past, only the teacher brought materials into the classroom, now students do so as well. They come to school bearing iPods and MP3 players loaded with text, images, and sound, vastly enriching the subject matter being covered in class. In schools that welcome such openness, the teacher is a mentor and facilitator rather than the guardian and purveyor of knowledge. The following is an example from a school that has embraced this new educational reality.

The room 208 podcast may just have the youngest production staff in the history of broadcasting. Written, produced, and performed by the third and fourth graders in Bob Sprankle's class at the Wells Elementary School in Wells, Me., the podcast—an online radio show that can be downloaded to an MP3 player—began in April, has 171 subscribers for its weekly 20–30 minute shows, and includes regular features like "Student News," "The Week in Sports," and "Word of the week.". . .

"In building this product weekly, the kids are incredibly motivated to read, research, write, and they're telling me they can't wait to get to school," Mr. Spankle said for the June 9 episode of Connect Learning, another podcast (not affiliated with his school). "You can't just fake it with this show; you have to own it."[1]

In many ways, new technologies have updated and revitalized John Dewey's concept of progressive education. Dewey was opposed to classical Latin School, pedagogy that emphasized the doctrine of formal discipline. According to this doctrine, learning Latin, Greek, and mathematics strengthens the mind. In contrast, Dewey wanted education to be functional. He wanted children to acquire the knowledge and skills they would need once they were out of school. Dewey's idea of education brought wood, print, and machine shops, as well as typewriters and sewing machines, into the schools. In addition, Dewey advocated the *project* method of learning. He regarded the distinction between academic disciplines as arbitrary. For Dewey, children learn best when they are challenged by a project that requires them to bring together a variety of skills. He contended that in putting on a play, for example, children learn about language and literature, learn how to sew costumes, build stage sets, and work together as a group.[2] Creating a podcast is a good example of the project method, albeit in a way Dewey couldn't have imagined.

Dewey's project method combines creativity, self-motivation, and practical learning—play, love, and work. Such education is effective because it addresses the child's heart, mind, and body. The pedagogical power of this integration is what I have been stressing throughout this book. Our new technologies are allowing children to revisit the project method in fresh and novel ways. Dewey, writing at the beginning of the twentieth century, wanted to school children in the knowledge and skills needed to survive and prosper in the industrial age. Similarly, at least one goal of contemporary education is to pro-

vide young people with the technological know-how needed to suc-
ceed in the information age.

The New Educational Reality

Our new technologies, as well as the permeability of the boundaries
of home, school, and world at large, have refurbished some of Dewey's
soundest pedagogical principles. Technology is creating a new educational reality. First of all, teachers, including college and university
professors, no longer have a monopoly on skills or knowledge. Regarding skills, young people have a facility with the new technologies
that is the envy of those who are many times their age. As to knowledge, thanks to a variety of computer programs, the Internet, and
search engines like Google, information on any subject is only a few
finger taps away. Further, the finest teachers—once limited to the students in their own classrooms—are increasingly available to all. You
can now buy an introduction on CD to almost any subject, taught by
some of the most outstanding professors in their fields. Moreover,
Phoenix University, headquartered in Phoenix, Arizona, and serving
270,000 students in 40 countries, offers a full college education using
interactive computer technology.[3] With the price of tuition, to say
nothing of room and board, continuing to rise at all schools, more
students may opt for an online education.

Second, the availability of so much knowledge on our home
computers underscores the truism that education has never been
limited to what is learned within classroom walls. When I was a
child, a library card opened up a whole new world for me. Every
Saturday morning I rode my bike to the local library to pick up my
quota of new books. Growing up in Detroit, my friends and I in-
herited a passion for cars and could name the make, model, and
number of cylinders for every car that passed by. We could also explain how internal combustion engines worked. That was then.

Today I take my granddaughters to children's museums that are fantastic places for exploration and learning through play. Learning outside of school has increased exponentially with the enormous technological advances of the past few decades. I am really impressed with the technologies my college students have learned on their own. For example, their take-home exams reflect Web research, and they use advanced Power Point presentations in their term projects.

Finally, schooling has also been greatly affected by the accelerating growth of scientific knowledge. By the time a contemporary middle school student reaches college, much of what she learned in biology, chemistry, and physics may be outdated. Textbook publishing cannot keep pace with the speed of accumulating information. More and more textbooks now come with CDs and links to Internet sites for updating. Textbooks are becoming a smaller part of a curriculum rich in media resources. Like the boundaries between home, school, and the world at large, the communication barriers between scientific research and its availability to students and the public are becoming more and more breachable.

Despite many admirable examples in both public and private schools, tremendous inertia exists in the educational system, which is at once political, social, and economic. Children in low-income communities may not have the technologies at home, while school computers are dated and often nonworking. In more affluent communities, tight school budgets may not allow for, say, Internet and wireless connectivity. And in all of our schools, otherwise excellent teachers may not feel competent or comfortable using the new technologies. Moreover, the current emphasis on testing and accountability discourages innovative, integrative teaching and emphasizes narrow, rote learning. Most curricula are increasingly test driven and offer few opportunities for children to create their own learning experiences, such as writing and producing a podcast. While some testing is useful and important, overtesting is the death of effective education.

Too many public and private schools have failed to embrace the new educational reality. Unlike many past educational innovations, such as the expensive reading programs that ended up on shelves in the school storeroom, the new educational technologies are here to stay. Computers nowadays are vastly different from the early teaching machines that had a brief heyday in some schools but were too cumbersome and limited to make a dent in the educational system. Some early computer programming for children, for example, computer scientist Seymour Papert's Logo, was ahead of its time.[4] Logo didn't take off, in part at least, because the technology Papert was using was still in its infancy. With their vastly increasing power, memory, and sophisticated programming together with decreasing size and price, computers are at the heart of the new world of education. They are what college students, and even students in high school and middle school, bring to school with them.

The new technological pedagogy is changing the relationship between home and school. As the boundaries between home and school become increasingly permeable, home and school are looking more and more alike. Whereas print media used to be the link between home and school, now the links are more numerous and electronic. The technology of the school is duplicated in the home with television, computers, printers, and fax machines common to both. Cell phones and e-mail make communication between teachers and parents, as well as teachers and students, possible at all times of the day and week. Parents can become more involved in their children's schooling than ever before. I will make some suggestions in regard to that involvement later in the chapter.

The Early Education Model

The discomfort with change, the rigid and test-driven curriculum, and the public schools' slowness to embrace new technologies contrast sharply with the kind of education young children are receiving in quality early childhood programs. They are child centered and play oriented, and employ the project method. Ironically, of all the educational models, the early childhood model is the one that is most in keeping with the new educational reality—even before the new technologies. Although it seems counterintuitive, quality early childhood education should be the model for education at all levels.

Early childhood education was introduced by French philosopher and social critic Jean-Jacques Rousseau in his classic book *Emile*. In his book Rousseau asserted that children have their own ways of knowing and thinking. He further asserted that adults should honor and respect those abilities and predispositions in their educational practices—what is today called developmentally appropriate practice.[5] His archrival, philosopher John Locke, took the opposing position and argued that "nothing is in the mind that is not in the senses." In this way he denied innate potentials and dispositions and insisted that nurture, not nature, should be the basis of education.[6]

The first early childhood educators—Johann Pestalozzi, Friedrich Froebel, and Maria Montessori—took Rousseau as their mentor and constructed programs for young children that were adapted to their emerging needs, abilities, and interests. They all recognized that young children primarily learn through play. Those concerned with primary and secondary education, however, followed the Lockean model. In the United States, with the introduction of universal public schooling in the 1830s, schools went in two directions: (1) The Latin School followed the ancient tradition of teaching Greek, Latin, and mathematics as a means of training the mind. (2) The factory model, reflecting the rise of the Industrial Revolution, looked at educating as progressively filling an empty slate.

In many ways Dewey's progressive education movement was an effort to make education more child centered and functional—more akin to quality early childhood education. The movement failed, in part at least, because the technology was not available to make it work. To fully implement the project method at the higher levels of schooling requires strong outside support that was not available to teachers in Dewey's time. By midcentury the progressive movement was no longer viable and a new academic emphasis became the norm. A number of educational reforms have failed to raise children's level of academic achievement. Indeed America continues to fall behind other countries in international comparisons.[7]

Although the era of oral culture was long gone by the nineteenth century, some of the learning and teaching methods of that era persisted into the culture of print. Memorization and rote learning, despite Dewey's efforts to bring the project method into education, were (and still are) employed to a much greater extent than is necessary. Technology can do most of the memory work for us. This is a familiar phenomenon: we never move abruptly from one technology to another. The same is true for our schools, which are still organized around the so-called Carnegie unit. Steel magnate Dale Carnegie suggested that an hour provides an objective measure of labor and a means of standardizing payment, namely, the hourly wage. Schools following the factory model also adopted the Carnegie unit.

As we move into the new technological world of education, the inadequacies of the factory model and the Carnegie unit are becoming increasingly apparent. Those who are willing to look can see that the early childhood model of education is best suited to meet the new educational reality. That is what makes contemporary efforts to impose the factory model of education onto preschool pedagogy such a travesty. Quality early childhood education is effective because it integrates play, love, and work. There are no Carnegie units and little rote learning and memorization in quality programs for young children. They themselves decide what projects they want to work on and how long they will stay with them. There are limits, of course, but the child's needs, interests, and ability level help determine the curriculum. Certainly there is a place for rote learning and memo-rization in education. Knowing the multiplication tables by heart is very helpful. Learning quotations, poetry, and song lyrics can also be useful products of rote learning and memorization. But such meth-ods should never be the primary or sole methods of instruction.

In primary and secondary schools where the new technological reality is gaining a foothold, the model is more like the early child-hood classroom. Young people in these schools have some input into the curriculum and have as much time as they need to com-plete their projects. The school is a starting point for their learning and exploration, but it does not confine them physically or intellec-tually. When children have a say in their learning, they are much more excited and involved than when they do not. The respect their teachers show them is reciprocated and is the basis for bonds of af-fection. Under these circumstances children learn the tool skills and knowledge about the world in a way that is enjoyable and has a last-ing impact.

Of course there are less positive aspects of this technological rev-olution too. Pornography, computer gambling, and Internet seduc-tion are a few examples of ways in which computer technology can be used for unhealthy purposes. If we are aware of the risks and take measures to avoid and minimize them, we can reap the educational benefits of the new educational reality. Yet it would be unwise to welcome this revolution without taking measures to reduce its po-tential risks.

The implementation of the new pedagogy in our public schools is moving slowly. Social revolutions can be brought about by new ideas or new technologies. In either case, it takes time for the old ideas or technologies to be uprooted. The idea that the earth revolves around the sun and that it is round and not flat took a long time to be ac-cepted. Darwin's theory as to the origin of the species is still being contested. The idea that early childhood education, with its union of play, love, and work, should be the model for all education is likewise meeting resistance by those wedded to the factory model of education. But technology will not be denied; as children and teachers become more adept with the new electronic media, a new educational model will replace the old.

Maria Montessori designed her educational methods for preschool children. But Montessori recognized that her approach could be used at all age levels and sketched out ways for doing so. A number of Montessori schools now go to the high school level. In the same way, Rudolph Steiner, the inventor of the Waldorf schools, designed an early childhood program that he later expanded. Both the Montessori and Steiner schools have have continued to grow in number for close to a century. These programs have survived and flourished because they maintain their own schools of teacher training. Teachers learn to create their own curricula, which frees them from the domination of textbooks. These programs were putting the principles of the new educational reality into practice long before the advent of the new technologies, and they were among the first to incorporate these technologies into their curricula.

The Early Childhood Model in Practice

Montessori Schools

Trained as a physician, Montessori did her early work with retarded children and used many of the materials introduced by Edouard Seguin—whom some regard as the father of special education. Thanks to Montessori's intervention, some of her supposedly retarded students were able to perform at grade level. Her work in this area received national and international attention. What interested Montessori, however, was not that the retarded could perform at grade level, but that many children of average or higher mental ability could not. She went back to the university to study education and hoped to start a school for children of average ability functioning below the academic norm. This was difficult to do within the confines of Rome's rigid public school system. She got her chance when the owners of a refurbished low-income housing project asked for her help. The landlords rented to married couples with about fifty preschool children. While their parents were at work, the children ran through the buildings, defaced the walls, and engaged in what little vandalism they could invent. The owners believed it would be less expensive to pay for a day nursery than to keep up with the damage. Montessori was asked to set up the nursery and she accepted.

At that time early childhood education was not widely accepted; most children did not start school until the age of six or seven. Montessori believed that she could educate young children using the simple materials she had adapted from Seguin and used successfully with retarded children. It was her belief that early childhood was a critical period for the education of the senses, which formed the basis for later symbolic learning. She firmly believed that if children were not allowed to develop their senses to the full, all subsequent learning would lack a firm foundation. Her emphasis on sensory education sets Montessori apart from other early childhood educators.

Montessori opened her school, the Casa dei Bambini (which still exists today), in the San Lorenzo section of Rome in 1907 with an untrained teacher and some materials she had adapted from Seguin. At the same time that she was running the school, she was also teaching at the university, working as a physician, and giving public lectures on suffrage for women. But she managed to visit the school and talk with the teacher almost every day. Each night she modified her materials and the procedures for using them. This research became the basis for the Montessori method of education.[8]

As news of her innovation and success spread, the school attracted visitors from all over the world who wished to imitate it. Montessori wisely established training schools and methods of certifying teachers. Her tight control over her methods and materials has been criticized, but I believe she was correct in her belief that the value of the educational program would be dissipated in the absence of strict controls.

Montessori's control over materials is one of the reasons for the late introduction of her method into the United States. She presented a model Montessori classroom at the 1916 World's Fair in San Francisco to great acclaim. A dispute about production of her materials and writings, however, left her without a publishing contract. Acceptance of her methods was also hindered by a well-regarded academic, William Heard Kilpatrick, who claimed her methods were not scientific and her results unsubstantiated. Montessori was rediscovered in the 1960s after the Russian success with *Sputnik* got Americans thinking seriously about early childhood education as a way of improving education in general. Because of the belief that Montessori education effectively trained children in reading, writing, and math, training classes were organized and Montessori schools began to open all over the country.

The materials and methods for using them that Montessori created are unique to Montessori education. They are the most comprehensive, the most thoroughly field tested, and the most long-lived of the early childhood educational programs. Montessori teachers receive extensive training in the use of manipulative materials. Such hands-on training is unmatched in most of our college and university teacher-training programs. A virtual walk through a Montessori classroom for three- to six-year-old children will give you a the flavor of the program.

The Montessori classroom is usually a large open space with many windows and low shelves along the walls. Arrayed around the room are a number of different-size tables and chairs built so that children of different heights can sit comfortably on the chairs and work easily at the tables. The classroom is divided into different interest areas identified by the kinds of materials on the shelves in that area—math, science, reading, art, music, and other subjects. Children choose what materials they will work with and do so alone or in small groups. They can work at the table or on small rugs on the floor.

Montessori believed that children have a natural disposition toward neatness and order. After children finish using the manipulative materials, they are expected to return them to the same shelves from which they were taken. The Montessori classroom is very ordered and organized and the children are relatively quiet, which some visitors find off-putting. The children work by themselves or in small groups and generally give their entire attention to what they are doing. Montessori believed that even young children have a long attention span if they are deeply engrossed in the work they are performing. Because her materials are self-correcting, they have the power to attract and hold a child's attention.

Although Montessori originally focused on young children, she also addressed the education of older children. A number of Montessori schools now go to sixth grade and higher. At the Whitby School in Greenwich, Connecticut, Nancy McCormick Rambusch extended the Montessori program to the older grade levels and added art and music, areas in which Montessori showed little interest. Rambusch started the American Montessori Society (AMS), which was at odds with schools that follow the traditional Montessori curriculum and belong to the Association Montessori Internationale (AMI). Rambush wanted to adapt Montessori so that children could move easily from the Montessori program to non-Montessori private schools or the public school system. Today schools in the AMI tradition adhere to the original Montessori program, whereas the AMS allows for more innovation and includes art and music.

All Montessori schools are not alike. The quality of any Montessori school depends on the headmaster and the teachers. Montessori schools also vary in the ages they accommodate. Some Montessori schools take infants and some include high school. Because Montessori was less clear about education at the higher grade levels, there is more innovation and variation among individual Montessori schools that include the higher grades. Unfortunately there has been little direct research of the effects of the Montessori schools on later achievement. That said, I can offer anecdotal evidence of the fact that children appreciate the value of a Montessori education: those of my students who have gone to a Montessori school are uniform in their praise. They also seem to be thankful for what they learned and for being given a standard against which to assess high-quality educational practice.

The Waldorf Schools

The Waldorf educational program was created by Rudolf Steiner, a multitalented Renaissance man who believed that science should be based on spiritual as well as material truths. Around the turn of the century he helped found Weleda, a company that promoted homeopathic and herbal medicines, a forerunner of homeopathic medicine. He also promoted biodynamic agriculture, now known as organic gardening. He was deeply concerned about the direction in which society was moving and felt that the modern devotion to science and reason led to neglect of the artistic and spiritual side of human nature. Like Dewey, he regarded traditional education as too academic and too narrowly focused for children to attain their full human potential. He saw science and the arts as different sides of the same coin and thought they should be integrated within the same educational curriculum.[9]

Steiner was given the chance to put these ideas to the test after World War I. The owners of the Waldorf Astoria cigarette factory heard him speak and were so impressed with his arguments for integrating the arts and sciences that they asked him to found a school for their workers' children. The first Waldorf school was opened in Stuttgart, Germany, in 1919; there are now more than eight hundred Waldorf schools worldwide. In setting up the Waldorf school, Steiner intended to devise an educational system that would integrate all facets of the human personality. Like Dewey, he advocated teaching methods that brought together the artistic with the intellectual, the humanities with the sciences.

Steiner's educational ideas were based on his observations and what he regarded as spiritual insights. He divided child development into three seven-year periods. He posited that from birth to age seven, children are natural imitators—their primary mode of learning. Apart from reading children fairy tales, academic learning must be kept to a minimum during this age period. He also believed that children should learn the alphabet and writing in first grade but should not get reading instruction until the second grade. Steiner's second stage of growth (7 to 13 years) is characterized by the centrality of imagination and fantasy, as well as the acceptance and emulation of authority. Steiner said that children should have a single teacher during this age period, with classmates as fictive siblings and the teacher as fictive, authoritative parent. Not until adolescence (the third stage) begins at the age of fourteen does the young person become capable of understanding the world intellectually and conceptually. It is at this age, he said, that young people begin to think critically and challenge authority.

Many of the ideas Steiner advocated are only now becoming part of conventional educational wisdom. The idea that children should be taught to write before they are taught to read (in the formal sense of phonics) is now a generally accepted practice. The idea that children should stay with the same teacher for a number of years is recognized in the concept of multiage grouping, where the same teacher has children from, say, kindergarten through second grade. Finding links between the arts and sciences, a major Steiner emphasis, is the aim of the contemporary integrative curriculum movement. Steiner also insisted on the value of stories, biography, and historical anecdotes as aids to learning and memory. This insight anticipated the contemporary recognition of the narrative nature of all disciplines.

There are other features that make Waldorf education special. At all age levels, children research, write, and illustrate their own textbooks. As they move through the grades, children learn progressively more complex craft skills. For example, they begin with simple whittling and advance to elaborate wood carving and woodwork. Music is introduced at an early age so that children learn to play simple instruments and progress to more complex ones. They learn to use their bodies to move in time with music and to express ideas and emotions. It is an educational program that melds play, love, and work, as I have advocated throughout this book.

Steiner is not without his critics. He spent the latter part of his life advocating a spiritual philosophy he called Anthroposophy, which emphasizes the centrality of the spiritual in human life. Much of Steiner's educational program was inspired by his anthroposophical thinking. In most Waldorf schools, however, this aspect of Steiner's work is often downplayed while his educational ideas, particularly the emphasis on bringing together art and science, are most evident in the schools. I love to visit Waldorf schools. I am often offered a piece of beeswax to mold while I sit in the classrooms or watch the children outdoors. The environment is always warm and inviting, and children seem happy to be there.

The Research Evidence

The effectiveness of play-based curricula has been demonstrated in many studies both here and abroad. I do not claim that play *explains* academic achievement, which is the product of innate ability, family and social circumstance, culture, and much more. Rather, I believe that combining play, love, and work is the *means* of successful academic achievement. It is when all three are brought together that children have the best chance of learning in the context of their unique personal circumstances.

Israeli psychologist Sara Smilansky carried out a number of studies in the 1970s and 1980s that demonstrated the power of sociodramatic play promoting positive intellectual and social development. Smilansky defined sociodramatic play as involving four elements:

1. The child undertakes a make-believe role.
2. The child uses make-believe to transform objects into things necessary for the play.
3. Verbal exclamations or descriptions are used at times in place of actions or situations.
4. The play scenarios last at least ten minutes.

In addition to these four elements, sociodramatic play must involve two children and there must be communication between them.

Smilansky and her colleagues observed and assessed the sociodramatic play of three- to six-year-old children in a number of preschools in Israel and the United States. The preschools were selected to sample children from different socioeconomic levels. Smilansky and her colleagues also looked at children's ability to organize and communicate their thoughts and to engage in meaningful social interactions. The relation of sociodramatic play to academic achievement was clearly demonstrated in one study that followed the children through second grade. Children who had engaged in dramatic play as preschoolers demonstrated superior literacy and numerical skills as second graders.

Smilansky concluded from her extensive studies of play and academic achievement that socio-dramatic play activates resources that stimulate emotional, social and intellectual growth in the child, which in turn affects the child's success in school. We saw many similarities between patterns of behavior bringing about successful socio-dramatic play experiences and patterns of behavior required for successful integration into the school situation. For example, problem solving in most school subjects requires a great deal of make-believe: visualizing how the Eskimos live, reading stories, imagining a story and writing it down, solving arithmetic problems and determining what will come next. History, geography and literature are all make believe. All of these are conceptual constructions never directly experienced by the child.[10]

Smilansky's work added to a well-established body of research which demonstrates that children's imaginative play is supportive of social, intellectual, and language development. For example, the Columbia Teacher's College team of Ginsburg, Inoue, and Seo found that incorporating learning materials into the play of preschool children facilitated their acquisition of mathematical skills. Because these activities invited the children's active engagement, they were motivated to attain complex concepts. A comparable study demonstrated that children's reading achievement was greatly facilitated when they were involved in imaginative play with adults.

Several studies have compared children who attended preschool with an academic orientation with comparable children who attended a play-oriented program. The results showed no later academic advantage for the children who attended the academic program. In addition there was some evidence that children who attended the academic program demonstrated higher levels of test anxiety, were less creative, and had more negative attitudes toward school than did the children attending the play program. The investigators concluded that since the academic program has no demonstrable benefits and a number of possible risks, there is little to defend it.[11]

Other investigations demonstrate that low-income children profit from attending a quality early childhood education program, particularly when the program is play based. In one study, children matched for IQ were placed in one of three types of preschool programs: a traditional play-based program, a Montessori program, and a didactic (emphasizing academic skills and rote learning methods) program. Traditional and Montessori preschool programs were more effective in promoting academic achievement than were the didactic preschool programs. The group differences in math and reading achievement favoring the children from nonacademic programs were still evident at eighth grade. Interestingly, the findings were particularly true for males—usually the hardest group to reach.[12]

There is, then, abundant evidence that play-based programs are at least as supportive (or more supportive) of academic achievement as are didactic programs. And they carry much less risk of creating anxiety and low self-esteem.[13]

Beating the System

Many parents can't afford a Montessori or Waldorf education for their children. They have to deal with the educational system they have, rather than the one they would like to have. It is hard (and often fruitless) to fight the system. Many parents write or e-mail me and ask me to support their protest against some objectionable pedagogical practice or policy. While I appreciate their belief in my supposed powers of persuasion, I have no authority in such situations. In fact, as an outsider, any recommendations from me might be resented and do more harm than good. Nonetheless, there are things parents can do at home to counteract some of the teaching practices that have yet to embrace the new technological pedagogy. Despite the public schools, it is still possible for parents to give their children educational experiences that speak to their hearts, minds, and bodies. Here are a few suggestions that allow playfulness and creativity where rigidity and practice still rule.

The Dumb Books Caper.   Most textbooks are not field tested. Nor are most of the worksheets that are issued for homework. Most textbooks and worksheets have errors, sometimes of fact, sometimes of expression, sometimes merely grammatical. A game you can play with your school-age children is the Dumb Books Caper. You and your child are the detectives trying to find the errors in the textbook or worksheet. You can make this the child's mission, if he chooses to accept it, or you can play it together. This game helps children think critically about books and recognize that what is written in a book is not necessarily right or true. It has the added benefit of helping children not feel at fault if there is something they cannot understand or something that doesn't make sense. After you find the errors, you can talk about how they were made and how they could have been prevented.

The Case of the Missing Use.   Thanks to test-driven curricula, children are increasingly taught to think convergently, in line with accepted facts and beliefs. Consequently schools offer little opportunity to think divergently, outside the box of conformity. The "case of the missing uses" helps children think creatively and imagine unusual possibilities for everyday things. Again you can play detective; say something like, "This paper clip was used to commit a crime. What was it?" It doesn't matter how outrageous the answer is, and that is part of the fun. The game can be simplified if you simply ask, "How many uses can you think of for this hat, cup, pencil, (and so on)?"

This is a good game to play during a car trip. Trying to find the missing use, or as many multiple uses as you can imagine, helps nourish the child's imagination and creativity and is fun in the process.

E is for Ending.   Sometimes when children are required to read a story and write a book report, you can play a different sort of game. "Can you think of another ending for the story?" Or you can ask a question directly taken from the story. "What if this hadn't happened or what if the character had said this?"

When children are asked to write alternative endings, they get the idea that the story is not written in stone, that it could have been written in different ways. This experience gives them a sense of literature and writing that is open and flexible. Sometimes you can play the game with possible real-life events. After buying a lottery ticket, ask, "What if we won the lottery? What would we do?" The point of this game is encouraging children to think of possibilities, of what might be rather than what is.

Breaking the Report Card Code.   Report cards often create tension and stress when they come home. You can help reduce the stress by playing the Report Card Code Game. Parents usually assume that they know what the letters on a report card mean. But do they? Does a child who gets an A know twice as much as one who gets a B? How much smarter do you have to be to get from a B to an A? If I got a C did I get it because I didn't know the material, I didn't read the question right, I had a headache when I took the test, or the teacher just doesn't like me? We take grades too seriously. They are ranks at best, and the same grade may mean very different things for different children. Trying to break the report card code provides as opportunity to talk about the relative value of grades. It is not meant to challenge or discount the teacher's assessment, but to help kids see the whole picture.

The Hidden Bargain. Helping children acquire computer literacy is one of the best ways to introduce them to the new educational reality. If your child knows how to do a computer search, you can enlist her help when you shop online. Let's say you need a new lawn mower. Ask your child to go online and search the products, get reviews and costs of the various brands and makes, and come back to you with a recommendation based on her research. If her research is solid and the conclusion makes sense, you can sit down together and order the product indicated by the research. This kind of search gives children practice in finding and evaluating data. It has the added benefit that it serves a real purpose and gives the child a sense of contributing to the family's welfare.

The Neighborhood Tutor. I have already mentioned curriculum-disabled children—children of good ability who are simply mismatched with the curriculum and are performing below their potential. When parents try to tutor their children in this situation, they often get emotionally involved and can make the situation worse. Try to find, say, a high school student who is recommended by friends or who lives in the neighborhood to tutor your child in a subject giving him trouble. To be effective, the tutor has to be at least four years older than the tutee—otherwise the child will not accept the older child's authority. Children like being tutored by a teenager. Most teens enjoy tutoring and often do a great job; they have recently gone through the material themselves and may be aware of some of the obstacles and roadblocks.

There are other things parents can do to enrich their children's school experience. In addition to some of the games outlined above, playing computer games with children can help sharpen their computer literacy skills. It also gives parents a sense of the kinds of games that are available. Good computer simulation games are both fun and instructional. The real world is important too, and the more outdoor activities you engage in with your children the better. Walks, bike rides, gardening, and so on, keep parents and children in touch with the natural world, a healthy counterpoise to the increasingly pervasive virtual world of our new technologies. The virtual world is exciting to explore, but it is most meaningful if we move into it with a solid grounding in the real world.

It is a testimony to the power and universality of play that it is as effective in the virtual world as is in the real one, and that it is as productive at school as it is at home.

Epilogue: Gifts for a Lifetime

We all have tragic events emblazoned on our memories. Many can still recall where they were the moment they heard of President Kennedy's assassination. Most can recall where they were when they heard of the events of 9/11. We also remember the powerfully happy experiences of our lives. Such experiences provide us with a scrap-book of memories that we can call on for support in times of stress. It is one last example of the power of play.

An article published in the August 1949 *Reader's Digest* gives a touching illustration of this point. The author, Frances Fowler, re-calls a wonderful spring day from his childhood, a fantastic day for flying kites.[1] His mother and sister became so entranced watching him and his brothers fly the kites that they left their chores and went outside to watch. His father interrupted his work to watch, and many of the neighbors came out to join the fun. Fowler describes the scene this way:

> There never was such a day for flying kites! God doesn't make two such days in a century. We played all our fresh line into the kites and still they soared. We could hardly distinguish the tiny orange-colored specks. Now and then we slowly reeled one in, finally bringing it dipping and tugging to the earth, for the sheer joy of sending it up again. What a thrill to run with them, to the left and to the right and see our poor earthbound movements reflected

minutes later in the majestic sky dance of the kites. We wrote wishes on slips of paper and slipped them over the string. Slowly, irresistibly they climbed until they reached the kites. Surely all those wishes would be granted.

We never knew where the hours went on that hilltop day. There were no hours, just a golden, breezy now. I think we were all a little beyond ourselves. Parents forgot their duty and their dignity; children forgot their combativeness and small spites. "Perhaps it is like this in the Kingdom of Heaven," I thought confusedly.

Although the kites were not flown for any other purpose than the sheer joy of flying them, they had a long-term meaning and value that could not have been predicted. The kite flying took place in the late 1930s before World War II. One of the boys who flew the kites served in the army and returned home after spending more than a year in a POW camp. When asked about it, he said that when things got bad, he thought about the day and the kites. It helped him get through difficult times. A few years after the war Fowler paid a sympathy call on a recently widowed woman who had also watched the flying kites. When he offered his condolences, the woman smiled and said, "Henry had such fun that day. Do you remember the day we flew the kites?"[2]

The memory of playful experiences, as well as the play experience itself, can reduce stress and provide comfort and reassurance. It is yet another example of the power of play. However, this power is threatened by the current emphasis on suppressing play in the service of work for both children and adults. Yet the separation of play, love, and work is a misreading of how our basic dispositions operate. It is only when we integrate play, love, and work that we, as children and adults, can live happy, healthy, and productive lives.

Acknowledgments

When I told my wife, Debbie, that the last draft of this book was complete and that it had been sent off to the copyeditor, she sighed and said, "Thank God, I have my husband back again." So I want, first of all, to thank her for her generous patience and support over the months that I was away mentally, if not physically, while working on the book. I also want to thank my sons, Paul, Rob, and Rick, and my daughters-in-law, Randi, Norma, and Adrienne, for letting me use examples from their own childhoods, and from those of their children, to back up points I was trying to make. Thanks are also due to my sister-in-law Donna and my niece Lara, for graciously allowing me to use anecdotes from their children in the book.

Doe Coover, my agent, deserves many thanks, particularly for helping me appreciate that a book about play would have more appeal if the ideas were presented in a positive, rather than a negative, context. Most of all I want to thank Marnie Cochran, the editor at Da Capo Press who helped frame the book from beginning to end. Marnie encouraged me to articulate my own theory of play, which became the central theme of the book. In addition, her gentle but critical editing served to control my many excesses. The book is more consistent, more tightly focused, and more readable as a result of her efforts. Last, but not least, I want to thank all those parents, children, teachers, and school principals with whom I have worked over the years. In many different ways they have all contributed to my understanding of the power of play.

Notes

Introduction

1. Hofferth, S. L. 1999. *Changes in American Children's Time, 1981–1997*. Ann Arbor: University of Michigan Press.

2. Sackler, D. 2001. *A National Action Agenda for Children's Mental Health*. Washington, D.C.: National Institutes of Health.

3. Board, N. S. 2004. *Science and Engineering Indicators 2004*. Arlington, VA: National Science Foundation.

4. Elkind, D. 1994. *Ties That Stress*. Cambridge: Harvard University Press.

Chapter 1

1. Schiller, F. 1967. *On the Aesthetic Education of Man in a Series of Letters*. Oxford: Clarendon.

2. Derrida, J. [1972] 1981. *Disseminations*. Chicago: University of Chicago Press.

3. Wilson, R. R. 1990. *In Palemedes' Shadow*. Boston: Northeastern University Press.

4. Callois, R. [1961] 2001. *Man, Play, and Games*. Glencoe, IL: Free Press.

5. For example, Millar, S. 1968. *The Psychology of Play*. Harmondsworth, U.K.: Penguin; Sutton-Smith, B. 1997. *The Ambiguity of Play*. Cambridge: Harvard University Press; Almon, J. 2003. "The Vital Role of Play in Early Childhood Education." In *All Work and No Play*, edited by S. Olfman. Westport, CT: Praeger.

6. Froebel, F. 2003. *Friedrich Froebel's Pedagogics of the Kindergarten; Or His Ideas of Play and Playthings of the Child*. California: University Press of the Pacific.

7. Montessori, M. 1964. *The Montessori Method*. New York: Schocken.

8. Freud, S. 1943. *A General Introduction to Psychoanalysis*. Garden City, NY: Garden City Publishing.

9. Seuss, Dr. 1963. *Hop on Pop*. New York: Random House.

10. McCourt, F. 1999. *Angela's Ashes*. New York: Touchstone.

11. Csikszentmihalyi, M. 1996. *Creativity*. New York: HarperCollins.

Chapter 2

1. Hofferth, S. L. 2001. "Children Spend More Time with Their Parents Than They Used To." www.umich.edu.

2. Kline, S. 1993. *Out of the Garden*. London: Verso; Seiter, E. 1993. *Sold Separately: Parents and Children in a Consumer Culture*. New Brunswick, NJ: Rutgers University Press; Cross, C. 1997. *Kid's Stuff*. Cambridge: Harvard University Press; Quart, A. 2003. *Branded*. Cambridge, MA: Perseus.

3. Oppenheim, J. 1987. *Buy Me, Buy Me*. New York: Pantheon.

4. Rosenfeld, A. W., and N. Wise. 2000. *The Over-Scheduled Child: Avoiding the Hyper-Parenting Trap*. New York: St. Martin's.

5. Montessori, M. 1967. *The Absorbent Mind*. New York: Delta.

6. Harlow, H. F., and M. K. Harlow. 1966. "Learning to Love." *American Scientist* 54: 254–272.

7. Marriott, M. 2005. "Gadget or Plaything? Let a Child Decide." *New York Times*, February 17, 32–33.

8. Marriott 2005.

9. Cross 1997.

10. Cross 1997.

11. Matthews, G. 1987. *Just a Housewife*. New York: Oxford University Press.

12. Cauchon, D. 2005. "Childhood Pastimes Are Increasingly Moving Indoors." *USA Today*, July 12.

13. Kline 1993.

14. Baudrillard, J. 1988. *Jean Braudillard: Collected Writings*. Stanford, CA: Stanford University Press.

15. "Barbie Dolls." 2006. www.historychannel.com/exhibits/toys.

16. Schneider, C. 1987. *Children's Televison: The Art, the Business, and How It Works*. Lincolnwood, IL: NTC Business Books.

17. Papert, S. 1980. *Mindstorms*. New York: Basic.

18. Bruer, J. 1999. *The Myth of the First Three Years: Understanding Brain Development and Lifelong Learning*. New York: Free Press.

Chapter 3

1. Ong, W. 1988. *Orality and Literacy*. New York: Routledge.

2. McLuhan, M. [1964] 1994. *Understanding Media*. Corte Madera, CA: Gingko.

3. McLuhan 1994.

4. Wright, J. C. H., A. C. Murphy et al. 2001. "The Relations of Early Television Viewing to School Readiness and Vocabulary in Children from Low-Income Families." *Child Development* 72, no 5: 1347.

5. Anderson, D. R., and R. Larson. 2001. *Early Television Viewing and Adolescent Behavior: The Recontact Study.* Boston: Blackwell.

6. Rideout, V. J., E. A. Vandewater, and E. A. Wartella. 2003. *Zero to Six: Electronic Media in the Lives of Infants, Toddlers, and Preschoolers.* Kaiser Foundation Report. Menlo Park, CA: Kaiser Foundation.

7. Wood, A. 2004. *Teletubbies.* www.pbskids.org/teletubbies/parentsteachers/progphilo.html.

8. Montessori, M. 1964. *The Montessori Method.* New York: Schocken.

9. Edwards, C. 2006. "Class, Take Out Your Games." *Business Week,* February 20, 70.

Chapter 4

1. Elkind, D., and R. Bowen. 1979. "Imaginary Audience Behavior in Children and Adolescents." *Child Development* 15: 38–44.

2. Elkind 1979.

3. Mintz, S. 2004. *Huck's Raft.* Cambridge: Harvard University Press.

4. Parsons, T. [1949] 1968. *The Structure of Social Action.* New York: Free Press.

Chapter 5

1. Britz-Crecelius, H. 1972. *Children at Play.* Rochester, VT: Park Street Press.

2. Hoffman, B. 1972. *Albert Einstein: Creator and Rebel.* New York: Viking.

3. Bruner, J. 1963. *The Process of Education.* Cambridge: Harvard University Press.

4. Healy, J. M. 2003. "Cybertots: Computers and the Preschool Child." In *All Work and No Play,* edited by S. Olfman, 83–110. Westport, CT: Praeger.

5. House of Commons. 2002. *Education Select Committee Report: First Report: Early Years.* London: HOC.

6. Tolstoy, L. 2000. *Leo Tolstoy's Writings on Education.* New York: Teacher's and Writer's Collective.

7. Greene, B. 1985. *Good Morning, Mary Sunshine.* New York: Penguin.

8. Britz-Crecelius, H. 1972.

9. Montessori, M. 1972. *The Secret of Childhood.* New York: Ballantine.

10. Almon, J. 2003. "The Vital Role of Play in Early Childhood Education." In *All Work and No Play,* edited by S. Olfman. Westport, CT: Praeger.

11. Freiburg, S. 1959. *The Magic Years.* New York: Scribner's.

12. Bettelheim, B. 1987. *A Good Enough Parent.* New York: Knopf.

13. Freiburg 1959.

14. Chukovsky, K. 1963. *From Two to Five.* Berkeley: University of California Press.

Chapter 6

1. Piaget, J. 1950. *The Psychology of Intelligence.* London: Routledge & Kegan Paul.

2. Piaget 1950.

3. Zion, G. B. 1951. *All Falling Down.* New York: Harper & Row.

4. Baker, B. 1977. *Young Years: Best-Loved Stories and Poems for Young Children.* New York: Atheneum.

5. Segal, M. 2000. *Your Child at Play.* New York: Newmarket.

6. Chukovsky, K. 1963. *From Two to Five.* Berkeley: University of California Press.

7. Almon, J. 2003. "The Vital Role of Play in Early Childhood Education." In *All Work and No Play*, edited by S. Olfman. Westport, CT: Praeger.

Chapter 7

1. Games Kids Play. 2005. www.gameskidsplay.net.

2. Piaget, J. 1950. *The Moral Judgement of the Child.* London: Routledge & Kegan Paul.

3. Strauss, A., ed. 1936. *The Social Psychology of George Herbert Mead.* Chicago: University of Chicago Press.

4. Cowan, E. 1974. *Spring Remembered: A Scottish, Jewish Childhood.* Edinburgh: Southside.

5. Opie, I., and P. Opie. 1969. *Children's Games in Streets and Playgrounds.* Oxford: Oxford University Press.

6. Stone, L. J. C. 1957. *Childhood and Adolescence.* New York: Random House.

7. Piaget 1950.

8. Piaget 1950.

9. Elkind, D., and R. Dabek. 1978. "Personal Injury and Property Damage in the Moral Judgment of Children." *Child Development* 48: 518–522.

10. Elkind and Dabek 1978.

11. Fine, G. A. 1987. *With the Boys: Little League Baseball and Pre-Adolescent Culture.* Chicago: University of Chicago Press.

12. Fine 1987.

13. Sherif, M., and C. W. Sherif. 1956. *An Outline of Social Psychology.* New York: Harper & Row.

14. Adler, P. A., and, P. Adler. 1998. *Peer Power: Preadolescent Culture and Identity.* Brunswick, NJ: Rutgers University Press.

15. Powell, M. 2001. *Fort Culture: The Hidden Curriculum of Recess Play*, 277. Lesley University.

16. Powell 2001.

17. Sobel, D. 1993. *Children's Special Places: Exploring the Role of Forts, Dens, and Bush Houses in Middle Childhood*. Tucson, AZ: Zephyr.

18. Sobel 1993.

19. Ung, L. 2005. *Lucky Child*. New York: HarperCollins.

Chapter 8

1. Michelli, J. 1998. *Humor, Play, and Laughter*. Golden, CO: Love and Logic.

2. Michelli 1998.

3. Michelli 1998.

4. Cosby, B. 1991. *Childhood*. New York: Putnam.

5. Isaacs, S. 1986. *Who's in Control?* New York: Perigee.

6. Felix, J. 1977. *Proud Parenthood*. Nashville: Pantheon.

7. Elkind, D. 1976. *Child Development and Education*. New York: Oxford University Press.

8. Bloom, B. 1985. *Developing Talent in Young People*. New York: Ballantine.

9. Bloom 1985.

10. Kramer, R. 1976. *Maria Montessori: A Biography*. Chicago: University of Chicago Press.

11. Bloom 1985.

12. Elkind, D. 1994. *Ties That Stress*. Cambridge: Harvard University Press.

13. Lasch, C. 1977. *Haven in a Heartless World*. New York: Basic.

14. NPD Group. 2004. *Eating Patterns in America*. Port Washington, NY: NPD.

15. Earle, A. M. [1899] 1993. *Child Life in Colonial Days*. Stockbridge, MA: Berkshire.

16. Dewey, J. 1938. *Experience and Educaton*. New York: Collier.

17. Engel, S. 1995. *The Stories Children Tell*. San Francisco: Freeman.

Chapter 9

1. Whitehill, E. T. 2005. "New Tools, Blogs, Podcasts, and Virtual Classrooms." *New York Times*, August 3, E8.

2. Universityofphoenix.com. 2006.

3. Universityofphoenix.com 2006.

4. Papert, S. 1980. *Mindstorms*. New York: Basic.

5. Montessori, M. 1964. *The Montessori Method*. New York: Schocken.

6. Harwood, A. C. 1958. *The Recovery of Man in Childhood*. Great Barrington, MA: Mytrin Institute.

7. Gibboney, R. A. 1994. *The Stone Trumpet*. Albany, NY: State University of New York Press.

8. Montessori 1964.

9. Harwood 1958.

10. Smilansky, S. 1990. *Sociodramatic Play: Its Relevance to Behavior and Achievement in School, in Children's Play and Learning*. New York: Teacher's College, Columbia University.

11. Hirsh-Pasek, K. 1991. "Pressure or Challenge in Preschool: How Academic Programs Affect Children." In *Academic Instruction in Early Childhood: Challenge or Pressure*, edited by L. Rescorla, M. Hyson, and K. Hirsh-Pasek. San Francisco: Jossey-Bass.

12. Miller, L. B., and R. P. Bizzell. 1983. "Long-Term Effects of Four Preschool Programs: Sixth, Seventh, and Eighth Grades." *Child Development* 54, no. 3: 727–741.

13. Hirsh-Pasek 1991.

Epilogue

1. Fowler, F. 1949. "The Day We Flew the Kites." *Readers Digest*, August.

2. Fowler 1949.

Other References

Belsky, J., and R. K. Most. 1981. "From Exploration to Play: A Cross-Sectional Study of Infant Free Play Behavior."

Christie, J. F. 1991. *Play and Early Literacy Development*. Albany, NY: State University of New York Press.

Developmental Psychology 17: 630–639.

Fisher, R. U. [1981] 1991. *Getting to Yes*. New York: Penguin.

Ginsburg, H. P., N. Inoue, and K.-H. Seo. 1999. "Young Children Doing Mathematics: Observations of Everyday Activities." In *Mathematica in the Early Years*, edited by J. V. Copley, 88–89. Washington, DC: National Association for the Education of Young Children.

Singer, J. L., D. G. Singer, and A. E. Schweder. 2004. "Enhancing Preschoolers' School Readiness Through Imaginative Play with Parents and Teachers." In *The Child's Right to Play: A Global Approach*, edited by R. F. Clements. Westport, CT: Greenwood.

Index